Through God's Grace Publishing
P.O. Box 18065, Irvine, Ca 92623

Book Layout ©2013 BookDesignTemplates.com
Dreamstime.com - "Fit Young Woman Pushing Fast Food" Photo
Cover Design by "Graphic_Enamel"-Independent Graphic Artist with
Picture composition consultant Marianna Wescott, mariannadeamz@gmail.com

Ordering Information:
Quantity sales. Special discounts are available on quantity purchases by corporations, associations, and others. For details, contact the "Special Sales Department" at the address above.

15 Minute Healthy Organic Meals for Less Than $10 a Day —1st ed.
ISBN 978-0692298992

Contents

Dedicated to my sons, that

they have a healthy future and to all

parents who are committed to the good health

of their children and to all those who

advocate for a healthy and just world.

CHAPTER ONE

Intro and Basics

Introduction

So you have decided to improve your health, but you may be a little confused. One week you read that Canola is the new health food and the next you find out that it is one of the main GMO foods, which is a cause for concern. One week you read that high protein is where it is at and the next you find out that meat is highly acidic, contributing to diseases like arthritis. It is all very confusing and you wonder "Who can you believe?" It is like having pieces of a puzzle without being able to see the whole pictures. This book puts everything into perspective and teaches you about health in a way that is intuitive. You won't need to memorize pages of facts. You will only need to understand the six basic guidelines that most experts agree that you need to follow in order to eat healthy. The principles are: (1) choosing organic; (2) eating low on the glycemic index; (3) having the right acid/alkaline ratio; (4) include the right combination of protein, carbs and vegetables/fruits; (5) staying hydrated and (6) exercise that you love to do. Obviously emotional and spiritual health are major contributors to overall health, but we won't be addressing these two aspects of health in this book. There are people out there who are in a much better position to advise you on that than I am.

This is not a cookbook per se. You can go online and find all the recipes you want and all you have to do to make the dish healthier is to use organic, whole grains and vegetables. However eating organic is only one principle. People have boasted to me how they are heating healthy because they drink a large glass of fresh squeezed orange juice in the morning. Given how high juice is on the glycemic scale, they might as well as have had a coke for breakfast. Or they tell me they are eating "healthy" because they bring high protein snack bars for lunch. However these bars are very acidic with lots of sugar and are full of GMO soy protein. There is so much food out there that is labeled "natural" and "healthy" that is full of sugar and is acidic and not healthy at all. By the time you are done reading this book and have made several of the twenty four main dishes that this book contains, you will understand what you need to do to build your health in a way that is intuitive, that you can make work for any lifestyle with food you love. While this book has recipes, the main purpose of the book is to teach you how to set yourself up so you can come home from work and have a balanced,

delicious, healthy meal in less than five minutes that won't cost you a small fortune. The purpose of the recipes is to provide examples of healthy meals so once you understand what is involved, you can adapt any recipe. You may not like the "American" type main dishes. If that is true, then read through the main meal chapters anyway so that you can learn a routine that sets up your week with the foods you like in an hour.

The book also encourages people to use Fair Trade products so that that we eat in a way for a more just world. I am not a nutritionist. I am a single mom who likes to feel good, who doesn't like having moody, cranky children to deal with because of what they ate and who needs lots of energy to be able to work and manage a family. In addition, I need to do it all on a budget. I have spent hours sharing with my friends and co-workers how I get it all to work. Once they tried my suggestions and felt better, many told me I should write a book. So I did!

So what got me interested in healthy eating? The answer is that twenty five years ago my husband got cancer and through diet change, exercise, returning to God, etc. he went into remission. At the time he became sick, I read everything on health. As a result I have the "big picture" so to speak which helps me analyze all the new information that comes along. I have bought many cookbooks. The problem is that so many of them are written by people who know how and love to cook. They were often complicated, time consuming and sometimes the ingredients could be expensive.

There are those of you who may be thinking, you are not that unhealthy, you just want to eat better. If that describes you, I challenge you to take the "true state of health" test. For one day, don't drink any caffeine or eat anything with sugar in it. If you are exhausted, that is the true state of your health. Your body is actually exhausted and the caffeine and sugar is masking that. An exhausted body may be a body that may be borderline diabetic or too tired to fight off diseases like cancer.

Given my commitment to good health and the fact that I worked long hours as a business manager, I had to figure out a way to eat well that did not take a lot of time. Then I had children, so I had to figure out a way to make the food taste like commercially prepared foods or they complained constantly. While I was okay with a gluten free quinoa muffin that was as dense as a rock, they were not going to eat one unless it was a light as what is sold in a bakery. So I had to improvise and still keep to my principles of a highly nutritious alkaline diet that was quick and fairly inexpensive. What I offer is what I found most of my friends wanted, which was a practical plan that they could use every day. Then they do what I do, which is once a month pull out a fancy cookbook and create something new that one can incorporate into their meal plan. You can find almost any recipe you can think of on the internet but the authors of those recipes were not necessarily designing their meal plans in a way that was healthy and balanced. This book will teach you that by simply adjusting ingredient portions or adding an alkaline side dish, you can make any meal a meal that builds your health.

If you are looking for nutritional data, there is lots of information on the web you can look up. This book will provide the bare minimum on nutrition, just enough so that the book makes sense. I am not qualified to give "health" advice. What I am qualified to do is to share with you a plan that I have found works. The purpose of the first part of the book is to quickly set you up with enough education so you will know what is important and can immediately improve your health. Very few people will read an entire 100 page book on health facts. Most people just want "the bottom line." One of the purposes of this book is to save you hours of research and experimentation that one would need to do to put together what is in this book.

If you purchased the print version of this book at Amazon, you can download the e-book for free. That way you have your ingredient list on your phone for when you go to the store. You can download the Kindle app to any device in order to read e-books. If you like the book, please post a positive review at Amazon. If the book did not work for you in some way, then email me at healthyorgancmeals@outlook.com and let me know how I can improve it. I want the book to work for everyone.

Fair Trade

Throughout the book are suggestions on where to purchase Fair Trade, organic food products. "Fair Trade" means no child or slave labor was used to farm the food or distribute the product. Child labor is often used in the agricultural industry. Our imported foods such as fish, coffee, sugar, tea, tropical fruits and spices are often produced through slave labor. If we all refused to purchase products produced by slaves, then 2/3rds of the world's 27 million slaves would be spared a life of misery. "Human Trafficking" is a hot topic. However, many people fail to make the connection that with their purchasing power, they can end labor trafficking. More on this in Chapter Twenty Two.

The Basics

If you come home from work starving you are not going to want to spend an hour cooking a meal, especially if you have young children who are clamoring for food. If you are single, you might just pull out some cereal and milk. However given how high cereal is on the glycemic scale, you will have a difficult time waking up the next day from low blood sugar. In addition, both cereal and milk are very acid. Acidic conditions invite disease and body aches and pains. For many working moms, they want a casserole they can pop in the oven when they get home, so they can relax. Then they serve their children that casserole full of salt, msg, preservatives and who knows what else. They may even feel guilty, but they are doing the best they can. This book shows you how you can come home from work and pop a casserole in the oven that is nutritious and free of toxins.

If there is a secret or "hot tip" to making this all work, it is that at all times you need to have in your refrigerator a cooked casserole that you can heat up, cooked spaghetti sauce, (or some other sauce) cooked brown rice, cooked oat groats, (whole oats) cooked beans, cooked chicken, hamburger patties and buns, eggs, cheese, milk, onions and a few fresh vegetables. You will put the casseroles together on the weekend, so you always have food you can grab and heat up in 5 minutes.

The scenario might look like this: when you come home from work you put together a "bowl" or burrito, like you find at so many restaurants. All you would need to do is put your double boiler on the stove and steam some pre-cooked rice, frozen corn, pre-cooked beans and pre-cooked meat in the same double boiler top. Just put in separate sections with the food touching but not mixed up. Go answer your emails or take a shower or talk to a friend. What I love about a double boiler and rice cooker is you can't burn the food. As a busy single mother who is always trying to do three things at once, so I can get it all done, I have burned a lot of food!

Then put your ingredients in a bowl or wrap in a tortilla. Add soy sauce, teriyaki sauce, salsa and/or avocado and you have a great meal. Even little kids love this meal. I had so much fun going from restaurant to restaurant and trying out their "bowls" and all their great sauces. Sauces are in Chapter Seventeen. If you want to try creating your favorite restaurant food, just google (name of restaurant) (name of sauce) and see if you can find a close copy of a recipe or sauce.

For another great meal, you could take out some chicken legs that you already pre-cooked, so all you need to do is barbecue for 10 minutes with sauce. While you are waiting for the chicken to be done, you can heat up a pre-cooked yam in your toaster oven and steam some vegetables. To set yourself up for another simple meal for later, you could take out some frozen cooked lentils or cook some in the morning. When you come home from work you would just add a couple vegetables, an ounce of chicken and while your soup/sauce comes to a boil, you can steam up some rice. Run the soup through a blender, add yogurt and curry and pour over the rice. Or eat the lentil soup as a soup and just add a slice of corn bread or a couple quinoa/millet muffins for your carbs. Both these meals are really filling and there are a perfect nutritious, delicious, acid/alkaline balanced meal that has the right amount of protein and will cost you less than $3, even if everything you use is organic. All the meals mentioned above have the right combination of protein, carbs and vegetables and are low on the glycemic scale. What about desert and snacks you ask? Well there are chapters for that, including one for chocolate lovers. Sounds like a plan, doesn't it!

You can teach your teens how to put together these meals. If you have young children, then you can teach them how to use a toaster oven so they are safe and you don't have to cook so often. Sandwiches are great, but not everyone wants a sandwich all the time and it is hard to make a truly healthy sandwich unless you are cutting up vegetables which you don't want young children to do. By the time my children were ten they could line the pan in the toaster oven with foil and put the ingredients for the bowl on the paper. Then they would take the tray out and dump in a bowl and toss the foil so I didn't have to scrub a pan. This way you don't have to worry about them catching anything on fire. The worse that can happen is they burn their fingers if they don't use a hot pad to take the pan out of the toaster oven.

You can use parchment paper instead of foil so you don't have to worry about aluminum, but if it touches the top of the toaster oven, it can catch on fire. (I know this from personal experience!) I need to relax on the weekends, so teaching my children to cook for themselves created a more relaxed weekend time for everyone. It also paid off in the long run. When they moved out, given they understood what is in this book they could afford to eat healthy.

What about "Scientific Studies?"

Here is the problem with scientific studies; they can't really isolate out what they need and because they can't do that, all studies can be disputed. For instance, there are claims that eating low fat diets and drinking water out of soft plastic bottles when you are pregnant can contribute to autism. The problem with their claims is that in order to get a definitive study, you would need to find hundreds

of people of the same age, living in the same area, eating the same food, drinking the same water, with the same stress levels, (meaning same amount of children, same incomes, same marital status, etc.) similar jobs, etc. Then the study would need to be conducted over many years. That scenario is probably not going to happen. For that reason, all studies have "holes" in them and can be disputed.

While I may provide links to some scientific studies I am not going to try and dispute different studies. What I am going to do is suggest you do your own research and make common sense decisions. For instance given that plastic and aluminum can pass through the blood/brain barrier, does it makes sense to eat food that has been cooked or stored in them? Given that the brain is 60% fat, does being on a low fat diet make sense, especially if you are pregnant? If you have ever been on one of those diets, most likely you felt very irritable because fat insulates your nerves.

Everything should be done in moderation and if your doctor recommended a low fat diet, it may be because you have been eating a high fat diet for so long that you need to get your body back in balance, so you should always follow your doctor's advice. Also with fat as well as with carbs you need to take into consideration that there are good and bad fats and carbs. A balanced healthy diet includes all the food groups in the right proportions. While we invite you to do your own research and draw your own conclusions, there is nothing in this book that we will recommend that would be considered controversial as we are not going to recommend highly disputed programs like high protein or fat free diets.

Your Mood and the Mood of Your Family

What about all the diagnosis for teens for bi-polar disorder and opposition defiant disorder? While they may have a chemical imbalance, if I lived on Chitos and Coke I would cry easily and be extremely irritable and angry. Once you make the changes recommend in this book, you will feel great and be far less "moody," because your body will be balanced. Foods that are toxic, acidic and high on the glycemic index will definitely affect your mood because it affects our hormones.

For instance, people with low blood sugar tend to feel depressed. There are studies that show that some types of pesticides block the production of serotonin (the feel good hormone) and melatonin (the sleep hormone). (1.1) (And you wonder why you are tired all the time and feel out of sorts!) I am not a scientist but it is only common sense that a hormone imbalance is going to contribute to "mood" disorders and a whole lot of other ills. Most families, when confronted with mental disorders find that they have a better outcome when they combine a good diet with counseling.

If you would like to avoid having cranky children, the secret is to always have food available that you can grab that will support their health. Teens need to have "fast" food available at all times. If they can't make it in under 5 minutes, they will find something else. At all times I have a casserole that they can heat up or the ingredients for "burritos" as outlined on page four. In five minutes you or your teen can have a two pound delicious, nutritious, organic, acid/alkaline balanced burrito or bowl that cost you @$4. Salsa and corn are alkaline. Beans and rice are mildly acidic. The meat should only be 25% of the burrito both for budget reasons and to achieve the correct acid/alkaline balance as meat is more acidic. (See Chapter Four)

Teens and men and woman in their 20's need to eat out as that is how they socialize and there are very few truly good choices. However if you fit in that category and can get a good breakfast in, a good lunch and/or snack like the burrito described above and a good dinner on most days then you are way ahead of the game as far as good nutrition goes. One of the best ways to get your children involved in eating healthy is to have them cook with you.

You children may start out like my teen did which was to complain on a regular basis "Do you know how much it sucks to have a mom who only has healthy food in the house!" My friends get soda, monsters, etc. and they are fine!" I learned from a brilliant therapist not to answer questions that are not asked or defend myself with my children. I didn't respond because he made a statement and was not asking a question. Then he said… "Don't you Care How I feel?!" To which I replied, "Yes, I care how you feel, but nothing will change regarding the food we have in this house because I am committed to good health." Of course he persisted, but I just kept stating, "We will not be discussing what kinds of food we will have in the house unless you are willing to work with me in having food that supports your health." Now two years later he tells me how crappy the quality of food is that everyone is eating and appreciates the fact that I have organic bread and peanut butter for him and organic noodles that he can heat up for spaghetti, etc. What changed his mind, you ask? Maturity and education. He finally came around.

References: 1.1 Study is here: http://www.mdpi.com/1099-4300/15/4/1416

CHAPTER TWO

Cooking Equipment and Your Food Budget

Microwaves, Pots, Pans and Cooking Dishes

An important thing to consider as part of your commitment to good health is the pots and dishes you use to cook in. While aluminum pots and pans are oxidized aluminum, if they get scratched you could be getting aluminum in your diet. Aluminum passes through the blood/brain barrier which could affect brain function. There are theories that there may be a link between aluminum in the brain to Alzheimer's. (2.1) While the theory is unproven, I don't want any aluminum in my brain, do you?

Teflon can also scratch, which may leach toxic substances in your food. Teflon also emits a gas that is somewhat toxic, especially at high temperatures. (2.2) When I was arranging to adopt a bird from my local bird sanctuary, they told me that before they let the bird in the house they were going to inspect my house for safety. Then they asked me if I had any Teflon pots in the house and they let me know that one pan would fail my inspection as cooking with Teflon can make birds really sick.

Yes, pots and pans are expensive so start with what you need the most. Get a stainless steel rice cooker. You can find them at Amazon and they only cost @$10 more than an aluminum one. Add a stainless steel pot, a double boiler and one pan. I bought a complete set for 70% off at an after Christmas sale because the set was going to be discontinued. Most superstores have stainless steel cookware for a great price. Non-stick "Green" cookware is becoming popular as it claims to not have the chemicals in Teflon. However you need fat in your diet in the form of healthy oils, which is why it is often recommended in this book that you sauté your vegetables with some oil.

What about microwaves? If you cook your food in water and toss the water, you will lose many nutrients which is why we recommend steaming, unless you are making soup. If you cook your food in a microwave with a container that has very little water with a lid, much of the nutrition is kept in unless the vitamins are of the type that are destroyed by the kind of high heat that microwaves produce. The biggest concern with microwaves is the containers people use to cook in. (2.3) Microwaves use high bursts of energy and often the containers people use have plastic in them which may leach into your foods. Personally I use a toaster oven with a pyrex dish (glass) or a ceramic dish to heat up my food so I don't have to turn my oven on. They are especially useful if you are single or just want to cook one cookie.

In addition to stainless steel pots and pans, you will need two pyrex dishes to cook casseroles. Having a cover for your pyrex dish is so great. When you are done eating, just snap on the cover and put in the fridge.

A crock pot is also a great time saver. You can make a stew in 10 to 15 minutes in the morning. Just cut up some vegetables, potatoes and meat.

Then add organic chicken or beef, some broth, a tomato, some basil, bay leaf, salt and pepper. When you get home all you need to do is add 2 TB flour mixed with a little water to thicken the stew, wait 5 minutes and serve.

The two most important "must have" items are a double boiler pictured above and a stainless steel rice cooker. With the double boiler you can heat up foods like cold, hard rice by steaming and it fluffs right up again. Or you can make sauces without burning them. I have forgotten that I was cooking rice and the rice has sat overnight in the cooker or all day and was still good to eat. A Food Processor, or what I call the "food chopper," will also save you a lot of time. I have the ability to buy organic, frozen, cut up vegetables so I rarely use a food processor except when I chop onions so my eyes don't water. If you don't have the ability to purchase chopped up vegetables or they cost too much, then consider getting a food processor as you will be incorporating lots of vegetables into your diet. You can buy a good size food processor for as little as $25. These processors chop vegetables really fast and make eating healthy so much easier.

Where you will need to spend some money is on glass containers to store your food. I don't trust plastic. Yes, they have identified the toxic chemical that leaks into your food when you store food in plastic containers and yes, they have taken BPA out of many plastic containers. However, they are always "discovering" that some new item is problematic and given plastic is made of chemicals, I don't recommend storing your food in it. The only time I store food in plastic is for dry ingredients like flour that will be stored in a cool cupboard.

Plastic

Plastic passes through the blood/brain barrier so it would be smart to not drink water out of soft plastic bottles. Most canned goods are lined with a plastic material. Have you noticed that almost all spaghetti sauce comes in glass containers. That is because cooked tomatoes are so acid, they eat into the liner and the BPA and resin can go into the food. As you peruse the web, you will find many recipes that call for canned tomatoes or stewed tomatoes but they are often sold in cans. The good news is that more and more food manufacturers have BPA free canned foods. "BPA Free Canned Foods" has list of companies that use BPA free cans (2.4) and you can always go to the website of your favorite brands to find out how they can their foods. You can make your own stewed tomatoes and freeze them in small glass containers so you have them when you need them. Also, while the U.S. does not allow lead in cans, other countries do so if you want to use canned food, it is not recommended you purchase anything made outside the U.S, Europe, Canada or Australia. (2.5)

With plastic, there are also environmental consequences to consider. The average family uses 1200 plastic bags a year and according to the Clean Air Council, 2.5 million plastic bottles are trashed every hour in the U.S. The United Nations Environment Program estimated in 2006 that every square mile of ocean hosts 46,000 pieces of floating plastic. There is a garbage dump full of plastic in the North Pacific Ocean that is twice the size of the United States! (2.6) So let's use re-usable shopping bags and re-usable glass water bottles whenever we can.

Your Budget

I know too many people who are broke who claim they need to live on Top Ramen. Top Raman costs @ 50 cents a package, netting 8 oz of noodles cooked. (We are not counting the water as that goes right through you.) In order to make comparisons, we are going to compare weight of food cooked. So Top Ramen would be $1 a pound. Organic cooked brown rice costs 75 cents a pound, cooked (3 cups) and is not acidic like white flour products. It is also clearly the better bargain in term of nutrition. Add sesame seeds and salt, delicious. You can also try butter, Soy Sauce, Tapatio, Kimchee or add in some beans, fresh salsa etc. so it comes to @$1 a pound, same as Top Ramen. I love fresh salsa with cilantro and brown rice. Soooooooooooooo good.

Not only is brown rice the better food choice, you will stay full longer because of the fiber. There is no fiber in flour products like noodles. In fact, you should avoid flour products if you are trying to lose weight as you will get hungry again very soon. Some people assume that eating healthy is expensive and don't even bother to really look into it. Also people tend to avoid change. Developing good habits is key to success in achieving any goal. The purpose of this book is to support you in doing that.

You may have been wondering......"How can one possibly eat organic for under $10 a day?" The answer is, you will need to cook from scratch. For those of you who don't know how to cook, don't freak out. You can always go online to find step by step videos and directions for basic cooking tasks. The meals are simple and easy to cook with most of them only needing a few ingredients which saves time. If you were thinking........... "This book is probably going to have me eating carrots and rice and

beans in order to eat for less than $10 a day," the answer is "not really." While some of the casseroles may have rice and beans in them, they also have other ingredients that make for hearty, delicious meals. Servings are from as little as $1 to $5 which is intentional so you have variety and can evaluate how to budget a meal. You can always eat one $5 meal and then later on in the day eat a $2 meal to keep within your budget.

The claim that you can eat organic for under $10 a day is based on eating one pound of food at each meal. That is what most women need. Children eat less. Men need more. If you need two pounds of food and you need to eat under $10 a day, then we will show you how to adjust the ingredients so you can do that. Raw, organic brown rice costs $1.55 a pound, yielding almost three pounds cooked. So if you are on a budget, get creative with beans and rice! If you are now thinking, "how boring," think again. Mexican food utilizes rice and beans. Indian and Persian food uses lentils, which is a type of bean to make delicious curry sauces and dishes. Whenever I would like to try to make a new dish, I google recipes from Asian, Indian, Persian, Greek, Vietnamese, etc. cuisines as they do wonders with rice and vegetables, making delicious healthy meals. I love the taste of turmeric, cumin and saffron which go so great with grains, beans and vegetables and are found in so many great recipes from around the world. After you have been cooking like this for a while, you may find the meat and potatoes "All American" diet very boring.

Throughout the book, I have provided a cost estimate for what most of the meals will cost using all organic ingredients. I used online pricing and rounded. In other words, 1 cup of raw rice makes 2.75 cups cooked, but I rounded to 3 cups to keep things simple and the difference is only a few cents. I didn't use store brands because they are often less expensive and I don't know what you have access to. In other words, Whole Foods has their own brand for Spaghetti sauce for @$3.50, while other brands are $4.50. Their coconut milk is $2.00. Other brands are $3.50. Hopefully you have access to store brands and Farmer's markets so your costs are actually less than what is quoted in this book.

The purpose of the "Budget" section is to give you an idea of what meals cost. Since costs can vary from store to store I recommend you watch your food costs and look for ways to save. For instance Chicken and Beef Broth is $4 or more a carton. You could use half the recommended amount and add water plus 1TB oil and some salt. It comes out almost the same in terms of flavor. I buy organic oil for $5 for 16 ounces. One Tablespoon is ½ ounce, so $5 divided by 32 is @15 cents a tablespoon.

Organic chicken thigh meat is $6 to $7 dollars a pound, organic breasts are $8 a pound. Organic hamburger is @$7 to $9 a pound. Stew meat is $10 a pound. If you only need hormone and antibiotic free meat, then you will pay $2 less a pound. For red meat I am basing my costs on "grain finished" meat which means the cow was grass fed until the last three months of their life. It is a much better tasting meat and cost significantly less than100% grass fed meat. While the grain phase is not organic, in my butcher's opinion the meat is still at least 90% organic. Given that a healthy body eliminates toxins, in my opinion there should be a very low percent of pesticides in this meat. However, let's be clear that this is both my opinion and that of my butcher. If you know of a study that has been done for pesticide content for "grain finished" meat, please do let me know and I will update this section. healthyorganicmeals@outlook.com

Organic Cheese is also @$7 a pound. Organic Fruit and Vegetables run from less than $1 to $3 a pound with berries being at the high end for $5 a pound. Three cups of organic grain or beans dry equals one pound. Three cups of raw organic brown rice weighs @ 1 pound. It makes close to eight cups cooked. So we divide $1.55 by 8, we get 19 cents. I am going to use 25 cents a cup in the recipes for my estimate on costs. Organic beans yield close to 3 cups cooked for each cup dry. They sell online for close to $3 a pound, so $3 divided by 9 cups is 33 cents a cup, so I am going to round to 35 cents a cup cooked. One cup of sugar weights about half a pound. I pay $2.00 per pound at Amazon buying the 5 pound bags. It is a lot more expensive if you don't and shipping is free for most orders over $35 so I take advantage of that. Just letting you know how I got the figures I am using. You will need to research what you actually pay and adjust. Hopefully it will be less than my cost estimates.

The four pound casseroles listed in our recipes are 45% grain/ beans/potatoes, 25% meat and cheese and 30% vegetables. So that is $1.50 for the two pounds of rice, potatoes and/or beans, $7 for the meat and cheese (1 pound) and $2.50 for the vegetables. The total is $11.00 divided by four pounds of food which comes to $2.75 cents for a one pound serving. Add in salt, cooking oil, catsup to eat it with, etc. and figure $3 a pound for a very healthy, acid/alkaline balanced, organic meal that includes the government recommended food groups. Figure @$3 for lunch and dinner, $2 for breakfast, 50 cents for your Kombucha or Kefir soda so you get your probiotics for the day and add in a couple snacks for $1.50, the total is $10 per day for an adult woman, half that for a child and $13 a day for an adult man.

You may be thinking……"if I eat a lot of grain how will I get enough protein?" In Chapter Four, we will show you that you are getting enough protein in a way that is easier on your body. Our bodies are not designed to eat a lot of meat or high protein diets. Meat eating animals like dogs have a much shorter and straighter intestinal tract, so meat can pass through quickly as meat can go bad after several hours in a warm environment.

If you are on a budget or trying to feed a large family and cannot afford the $10 a day or if your meat prices are significantly higher than what I have quoted, then you need to change the portions so you are using more grain and beans. You can use a little salsa, chicken broth, cream of chicken soup, etc. to flavor rice and beans.   Throughout the book, we will show you how to do that and you will discover how really good rice and beans can be.   Many cultures like the Indian, Asian and Persian cultures do a fabulous job of flavoring grains and vegetables while using very little meat, which is the most expensive item.   Health wise, Americans eat way too much meat.

In addition, throughout the book I will give you tips on how to save money. In the organic section, we will outline which foods absolutely have to be organic like strawberries and corn and which foods have less pesticides, so if you have to choose to only buy some of your food organic, you can choose wisely. The number one money saver is to not waste food. If it is nearing the end of the week and you still have not eaten it, then eat the leftover casserole for breakfast. You can freeze fruit, vegetable and meat before it starts to go bad.   Grains and pasta do not freeze well even if you try steaming them to rehydrate them. However, you can use frozen grains for soups.

Your doctor will probably tell you that a meat and potato diet is not that healthy and would probably be pleased that you are heading more towards a grain and vegetable diet, as long as you don't overdue the carbs. Processed foods and baked goods like granola bars, crackers, cakes, pizza dough, pie crusts etc. is what is going to cost you the most in a health food store. If you haven't been able to find those foods or have been avoiding buying them because of the cost, the good news is that you can make them organic and wheat free for pretty much the cost of the flour which is less than $3 a pound. You only need half a pound of dough to make a large pizza crust.

A really great way to save money is to grow your own sprouts.   The seeds cost pennies and all you need is a jar with a screen or cheesecloth on top. Sprouts are high in vitamins, minerals and enzymes. You can sprout most beans, some nuts like almonds and many seeds.   You can google "sprouting" to get ideas.

References: (2.1) Web.MD "Understanding Alzheimer's Disease -- the Basics"

(2.2) www.greenhealthwatch.com/newsstories/newslatest/latest0701/frying-pan-teflon.html

(2.3) CNN.com "Does microwaving food remove its nutritional value?" by Bob Barnett 2.7.14

(2.4) www. bpafreecannedfood.wordpress.com/bpa-free-canned-food-brands

(2.5) www.oregonlive.com/fooddday/index.ssf/2013/07/bpa_in_canned_food.html "Just how dangerous is BPA in canned food, and 10 ways you can reduce your risk of exposure." by Grant Butler, 7.30.2013

(2.6) Courier Mail.com AU, Floating Rubbish Dump in the Pacific Ocean, bigger than the U.S. Xavier La Canna AAP, February 03, 2008

CHAPTER THREE

Eating Healthy

How Important Is It to Eat Organic?

Okay, so you know it is probably not a good idea to overwhelm your body with pesticide poisons, but you look at the prices on organic food and you get a little overwhelmed. Many of the meals recommended in this book will consist of grains and beans and the difference in the cost between organic and non-organic is very little, especially if you are comparing them cooked. You will only save 15 cents a cup if you purchase non-organic rice and beans. Where you are going to spend the most money is on organic meat and organic fruit. So is it worth it?

The Newcastle University Study (3.1) compared 343 studies/papers comparing organic to non-organic. One of their findings was that by switching to organic fruits and vegetables, it was equivalent to eating one or two more portions of fruit and vegetables a day in terms of nutrition. Organic vegetables do cost more than non-organic, but many vegetables don't cost that much to begin with so consider spending the extra money for organic vegetables. For meat, try to at least buy hormone and antibiotic free. Chicken, even organic chicken is put in a chemical bath to kill bacteria, so make sure you wash it. If money is not a major consideration for you, then purchase "air dried" organic chicken which means the chicken was not put in a chemical bath.

According to USDA data on pesticide residue in 48 fruits and vegetables, the fruits and vegetables that you should always purchase organic, as they have the most chemical residue are the following: apples, strawberries, grapes, celery, peaches, spinach, sweet bell peppers, (imported) nectarines, cucumbers, cherry tomatoes, (imported) snap peas and potatoes. Coffee is one of the most sprayed agricultural products in the world, so you definitely want to drink organic coffee. Since the coffee industry employs child and slave labor please look for Fair Trade, organic coffee. If you need to compromise and purchase some foods that are non-organic, these are the foods lowest in pesticides: sweet potatoes, cauliflower, cantaloupe, grapefruit, eggplant, kiwi, papaya, mangoes, asparagus, onions, frozen sweet peas, cabbage, pineapples, and avocados. (3.2)

Many of you may have read all the conflicting studies regarding organic vs non-organic and you

aren't sure what to believe. Some studies claim that non-organic foods, especially GMO foods cause cancer and all kinds of health problems. Other studies claim that our bodies can easily handle low levels of insecticides, but wouldn't you rather avoid them altogether? Your immune system is fighting environmental pollution like smog, daily stress, etc. every day. Eating foods with insecticides adds to the "workload" of your immune system. Personally, I want my immune system to be freed up from having to handle toxins in my food, so it doesn't get overloaded and I wind up getting sick. Everyone has cancer cells in their body which your immune system destroys every day. When the immune system becomes weak and can no longer destroy the immature cancer cells, they start multiplying at an alarming rate and crowd out healthy cells creating many health problems.

The main GMO foods are corn, soy, canola, sugar beets and cotton. So you don't get confused, hybrid means two foods were crossed together. Genetically modified (GMO) means that the insecticide is in the DNA of some foods, so it can't be washed off. For other foods, it means that the seeds are "pesticide resistant" meaning that the plant can handle a greater pesticide load. (3.3) Since oil is the essence of food, you are getting GMO in all your non-organic corn, vegetable and canola oil. If you read your labels you will find that most "vegetable" oil is made up of corn and canola oil. Keep in mind that there is opposition to the studies that claim that GMO foods deplete the immune system and can cause diseases like cancer. You are welcome to do your own research. I always take into account who did the study and if they have a financial interest in the outcome. While the effects of GMO foods are continuing to be re-searched, countries like Russia and France have decided to err on the side of caution and not allow GMO foods in their county until studies prove GMO's are harm less. In the U.S. we decided to wait until it was proven that GMO foods cause health problems before we eliminated them. So what position do you want to take?! At the very

least, please use only organic baby formula as corn syrup and soy, two of the top GMO foods are used in many baby formulas. Since baby's bodies are smaller the effects of toxins can be more pronounced. (3.4)

So is it really worth the money to eat organic? Disease, hospital stays, etc. are very, very expensive and that is not counting the time missed at work. Dealing with a sick child can be heartbreaking. On the other side, having a great sense of well-being from eating well makes all of this, well worth it.

Acid/Alkaline Balance

Disease and arthritis love acidic environments. When the body's fluids become too acidic, minerals are pulled out of bones, teeth and tissues to compensate which obviously weakens the body. (3.5)Acid foods also tend to make one irritable and can make your body hurt. If you are familiar with Macrobiotics, you already know that that way of eating recommends the 40% grain, 5% fat in the form of oils, dairy or vegetables like avocado; 25% meat/cheese/eggs and 30% vegetable ratio. That ratio is the perfect balance for an acid/alkaline diet which may be the reason why the Macrobiotic program works so well. People swear by the program's health benefits. Macrobiotics balances food according to Yin and Yang which is a close approximation of acid/alkaline balance. Yang is meat and dairy and acid. Grains, beans and potatoes are in the middle of the acid/alkaline chart. Vegetables and fruits are Yin and alkaline. Proponents of alkaline diets recommend that 70% of the foods you eat fall in the alkaline category. Many find that expensive and time consuming, but it is something to aspire to. What is interesting is that while coffee and tea are acid, green tea is alkaline. Here is a web link with a chart. www.mindbodygreen.com/0-5165/Alkaline-Acidic-Foods-Chart-The-pH-Spectrum.html

People who grew up in the Western countries such as the U.S., Canada, etc. don't always want to eat Asian type meals of rice and vegetables. They want hearty casseroles and meat loaf which is what this book provides. This book is designed for the meat and potato eater who is not interested in strict diets like raw food diets but want to improve their health. However, many doctors out there like Dr. Mercola recommend a lower percent of grains, down to 25% and incorporating more vegetables and fats in your diet in the form of healthy fats like avocado. A lot of it depends on how active you are. If you sit all day or have low blood sugar, you need less carbs. If you have been eating too much of anything, like carbs for a long time, you may need to eat a lot less for a while until your body comes into balance.

The Paleo diet and many other high protein diets gain popularity from time to time, but you will find very few doctors who think high meat diets are healthy. They are very acidic. If you want to be on a high protein diet in order to lose weight, just make sure that at least half of your food is alkaline which will consist mainly of vegetables. (http://greenopedia.com/article/alkaline-food-chart-degree) I was getting arthritis in my neck and my knuckles were starting to swell, so I cut down on coffee (acidic), took out almost all sugar (very acidic) and cut down on meat (acidic). All my symptoms disappeared. When I occasionally get arthritis in my neck or a headache, I avoid caffeine and eat green salads with lemon juice (very alkaline) dressing, drink water and all symptoms shortly disappear.

The Glycemic Index

The Glycemic index measures how fast our bodies metabolize food. It only takes your body about two to five hours to use all of the energy and nutrients from fruits, vegetables and starches. (3.6) However sugar and raw juice can take as little as 15 minutes, which is why orange juice can have the same impact on your blood sugar as a coke. Why this is a problem is that foods high on the glycemic index can metabolize so fast that your blood sugar can become dangerously high. In order to bring your body into balance, your pancreas needs to secrete insulin to bring your blood sugar down. However it goes so low that you have another dangerous condition. So your adrenals have to get involved in order to get your blood sugar back up again. This process exhausts your pancreas and adrenals and you wind up with low blood sugar and/or diabetes which simply means your pancreas is so exhausted, it can't make insulin anymore so you have to administer chemical insulin to keep your blood sugar from becoming dangerously high.

Fat and protein take about 12 hours to completely metabolize, with your body using the protein first. Once all of those calories have been used, you begin to metabolize the fats. (3.5) If your adrenals and pancreas are exhausted you will actually feel better on a high protein diet, as high protein diets don't involve the work of your adrenals and pancreas to manage blood sugar because meat is low on the glycemic scale. If you are eating high on the glycemic index, most likely you will be exhausted all the time because your blood sugar is low, especially if you eat high on the index before you go to bed at night. So eat very little foods high on the glycemic index for dinner. Potatoes are a good example of what to eat in moderations as they are 85 on the index, 21 on the glycemic load for one serving.

Eat your sweets during the day if possible. Here is a link for the Glycemic Index with a food chart. www.health.harvard.edu/newsweek/Glycemic_index_and_glycemic_load_for_100_foods.htm   However, it is not practical to memorize a list.   Just remember that all sugar, fruit juice and white flour products like processed cereals are high on the index.   Whole grains, most fruits and starchy vegetables are in the middle. Non-starchy vegetables like green leafy vegetables are very low on the index. So is meat and nuts.

Note that complex carbs, like brown rice are 16 on the glycemic load chart but white rice is 43 per serving or 2.5 times higher than brown rice. This is an example of how processing food drives up its score on the glycemic index. If you are overweight or tired a lot then reduce your carbs to 120 grams a day if you are a woman. Size and gender effect quantity, so experiment as to how many carbs are too much. Personally I try to stay under 150 grams of carbs a day as I am not that active and I gain weight if I eat more. A cup of rice is 45, a cup of beans is 37 and a cup of sugar is 200 grams of sugar. No, that is not a typo. A 32 ounce drink has a little over ½ cup of sugar in it which is why for soda drinkers, diabetes is in your future. In order to reduce your carbs, you will need to eat more vegetables, meat and beans. Wait you say, what about acid/alkaline balance? When I say "eat more," I mean slightly more meat. You can eat as many vegetables as you need. Everyone needs to eliminate sugar, fruit juice and sports drinks. Drink Kefir Soda and Kombucha instead which are both probiotic drinks with very little sugar.   The bottom line is you need to avoid foods high on the glycemic index and when you do eat them it should be in small quantities. How you combine your foods is also important. It is much better to eat cake than candy, as whole grain cake will have more complex carbs and protein in the form of eggs and milk that can slow down the metabolism of the sugar.

Sweeteners

There are many articles on the web that claim that cancer loves sugar and how sugar depletes your body of B vitamins. Even if you are not diabetic, you should try and reduce your sugar intake as much as possible. If your doctor has told you that you cannot eat sugar because you are diabetic, then look at the ingredients for everything you use and substitute. For instance, catsup can have more sugar proportionally than ice cream, so for recipes that include catsup put tomatoes in a blender and cook with a little vinegar, salt and stevia and put in a jar for future use. You can find recipes online. If you are diabetic, most likely your doctor has explained the glycemic index and you are a pro at this. With regard to all the artificial sweeteners out there you can do your own research by googling "Is (fill in the name of the artificial sweetener) good for you?" After you have read the articles, you will most likely agree that it is not a good idea to use artificial sweeteners other than Stevia.

Stevia is made from a plant and is not processed the same way other artificial sweeteners are. Stevia is 100 times sweeter than sugar. You can substitute 1/3 tsp Stevia for ¼ cup sugar. Some Stevia has fillers packed with it, so you need to experiment to find what amount works best.   Stevia does have a bitter aftertaste and you most likely won't like food that only has Stevia in it. Honey helps cover the bitter aftertaste but for some foods like chocolate chip cookies, most people don't want to taste honey as they aren't use to that taste for chocolate chip cookies. You can also try rice syrup as a sweetener. In an effort to reduce your sugar consumption and avoid exhausting your pancreas and adrenals, all recipes call for Stevia and a reduced amount of sugar than what would normally be called for. For your favorite recipe, for each cup of sugar it calls for, use ¼ tsp Stevia, 1 TB honey and ½ cup sugar or no honey and ¾ cup sugar. Start here and you won't notice any difference in the taste. Then over time, keep increasing your Stevia intake and reduce your sugar intake. If you have been told by your doctor to not use sugar at all, ask your doctor if you can use ½ tsp Stevia and 1 TB Honey in a recipe like chocolate chip cookies. The sugar free chocolate chips mostly use artificial sweeteners, so don't use too many chocolate chips unless you can find chips sweetened with Truvia. However, some people are suffering adverse reactions to Truvia that they did not have with Stevia. You can search the web for "Truvia side effects" and decide for yourself how you feel about this sweetener. Even Stevia should be taken in moderation.

According to the U.S. Center for Disease and Prevention, Diabetes affects 9.3% of Americans with another 27% at risk. That is almost 40% of our population! Don't you think we should be making reducing sugar and simple carbs a priority before we go bankrupt trying to treat this disease?!

Diabetes is another reason to go organic as studies have found that he rbicides (pesticides) block the body's ability to make insulin and could be another contributor to diabetes. (3.7) Even if you don't get diabetes, low blood sugar from exhausted adrenals is no fun either. Many people who have low blood sugar suffer from depression. If that is you, then aggressively work to curb sugar and high glycemic foods and see how you feel in a week.

References:(3.1)"www.ncl.ac.uk/press.office/press.release/item/new-study-finds-significant-differences-between-organic-and-non-organic-food" Newcastle University Press Office

(3.2) U.S. News & World Report on MSN Money "10 Ways to Save Money on Organics" By Laura Harders, 4.2014

(3.3) http://whfoods.org/genpage.php?tname=george&dbid=207

(3.4) http://pediatrics.aappublications.org/content/130/6/e1757.full

(3.5) Bottom Line Secrets, Is your body too acidic?
www.bottomlinepublications.com/content/article/natural-remedies/is-your-body-too-acidic

(3.6) www.healthyeating.com What Metabolizes Faster - Fat or Protein? by Maia Appleby

(3.7) Study: http://www.mdpi.com/1099-4300/15/4/1416

CHAPTER FOUR

Nutrition

Protein

If you combine beans or seeds with grains, you will get a complete protein. However according to Matt Frazier in his article "Protein, a Primer for Vegetarians," the body stores amino acids and uses them as needed so there is no need to stress over making sure your food combinations are working to get the correct amino acid ratio. (4.1) Do make sure you are getting the protein you need each day. A 3 oz chicken breast is 20 grams. 1 oz of sesame seeds or most type of seeds and nuts is 5 to 6 grams. So ounce for ounce, seeds and nuts are almost the same protein count as meat/cheese. One cup of cooked brown rice is 5 grams. A cup of cooked beans is 12 to 14 grams. Lentils are 18 grams. A cup of tofu is 20 grams. Peas, potatoes and spinach have 3 grams of protein per half cup. So the casserole we outlined with 40% grain/beans and 25% meat/cheese would be a total of @110 grams of protein divided by 4 servings is 30 grams per serving. To determine your protein needs, multiply .36 by your ideal body weight. Generally speaking women need 46 grams and men need 52 grams of protein per day. If you are an athlete, you need significantly more. On a typical day, a one pound serving of the casserole (lunch and dinner) is 60 grams of protein. Add in a protein shake in the morning and you are more than covered. For body builders your protein requirement is two to three times that of an average man or woman. Since protein is more expensive than carbs, you won't be able to stay within a budget of $10 a day, but you already knew that, right?!

As you can see from the chart from the next page, the proportions we recommend from the acid/alkaline chart are very close to what the experts are recommending for food portions. The difference is that our chart is lower on dairy and higher on meats. If you are concerned about getting the nutrients available in dairy, you can adjust your portions so you are adding more dairy and less meat, however many people do not tolerate dairy well and you can get a significant amount of calcium simply by eating more leafy vegetables and sprinkling sesame seeds on your rice. Sesame seeds are truly a "power" food. 2 TB provides 18% of your daily requirement for calcium and your daily requirements for the following vitamins and minerals: 80% copper, 23% magnesium, 16% phosphorus, 15% magnesium, 15% iron, 13% Zinc, 12% molybdenum, 12.5% of vitamin B1, 11% of selenium. (4.2) One of the reasons why the macrobiotic diet is so healthy is because to season the rice, it is recommended that one add 2 TB of sesame seeds with a little salt to each portion, for each meal. Sesame seeds also go great with vegetables. Best to store them in an air tight container in the freezer so they don't get rancid. Sprinkling sesame seeds on your food is a very good habit to get into.

Absorbing Nutrients

It is important to consume some sort of probiotic every day to aid in digestion so we get the most out of our food. As we age or if our bodies are weak, sometimes we may not produce enough enzymes to assimilate the nutrition in our food. It is a good idea to see a chiropractor who practices kinesiology so they can test you. You may need hydrochloric acid which is a very inexpensive supplement. A doctor can run tests, but that tends to be more expensive than the cost of a doctor visit to a chiropractor. If you are eating well, getting a full night's sleep, exercising and have a minimum amount of stress, you should feel really great. If you don't, then look into making sure you have the digestive enzymes you need for your diet to benefit you in the maximum way and make sure you are including probiotics to support digestion and good bacteria in your diet.

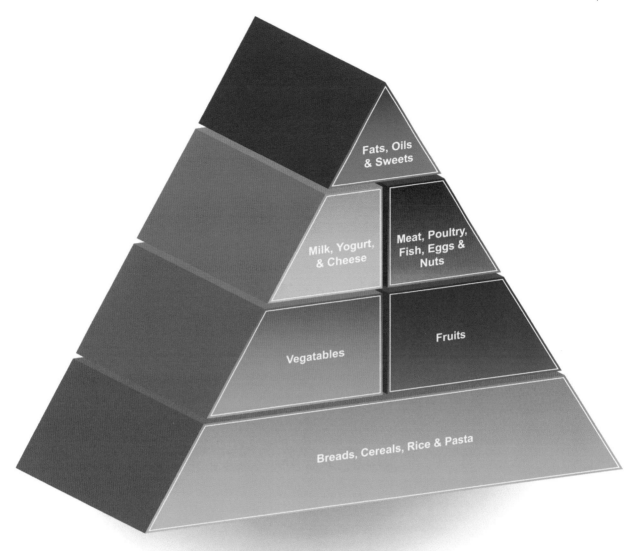

Currently there is a debate as to whether organic foods have more vitamins and minerals than non-organic. Nutrition has a lot to do with the quality of the soil where the food is grown. However, MDPI has a study that shows that pesticides deplete the body of vitamins and minerals because they destroy gut bacteria that you need to absorb nutrition. In addition, their study found that glyphosate (a chemical in pesticides) blocks the absorption of minerals. (4.3) So even if the nutritional value is the same going in for both organic and non-organic, your body assimilates more nutrition from organic foods. Also a body broken down by toxins is a body that is not as efficient at making the most of the nutrients you take in than a body that is healthy. Since you aren't in a position to determine how many vitamins and minerals your food has, it is always a good idea to take a supplement so you get what may have been missing in your food that day.

In the cooking sessions that follow you are going to make two to three times what you need for several dishes like chili and you will freeze the rest. Doesn't freezing affect the nutrition you ask? The answer is that many nutrients will be destroyed by cooking anyway. Most of the vitamins and minerals that aren't destroyed by heat won't be destroyed by freezing either. You will only freeze that which freezes well like spaghetti sauce, beans, etc. Making up food that you can just pull out of the freezer and make a meal will save you a lot of time and for many, having healthy food available that they can eat within 5 minutes can make the difference between having a meal with healthy ingredients or eating junk food. At almost every meal you can include a freshly steamed vegetable or raw vegetable that will take care of many of your nutritional needs and make your meals more alkaline.

Water

It is important that you drink water when you first get up because you are dehydrated. Try drinking a large glass of water, then getting in the shower so your body has a chance to hydrate before you drink your coffee. You may find that you are as alert from half a cup of coffee if you hydrate first, than from the full cup. One of the problems with caffeine is that it is a diuretic and can dehydrate you. I recommend you google your coffee brand as many have three times the caffeine of regular coffee which means you will need even more water to prevent dehydration. Given that most people wake up dehydrated and then drink coffee, they can become even more dehydrated which may be one of the reasons they are tired and feel out of sorts. The U.S. law that defines "safe" water is over 35 years old and doesn't take into account the tens of thousands of chemicals that have been introduced into the environment since then. (4.4) It is important that you use some type of water filter system. Many systems waste a lot of water, so do your research before you buy. For reverse osmosis systems, it is important you add back the minerals to the water with a pinch of Himalayan pink salt.

Dairy Free

Dairy products are very acidic and for many people, hard to digest. You can substitute your favorite non-dairy product such as organic soy, almond, rice or coconut milk for any recipe. You can use non-dairy, organic, non-hydrogenated Earth Balance butter as a substitute for butter. These products are far more alkaline than milk. Coconut milk works well in baked goods. I put "coconut" in parenthesis to remind you that you can substitute. For your coffee or tea most likely you will prefer almond milk. To make any item, you need the unsweetened variety or your dishes will come out too sweet. If you can only get sweetened, then taste your baked goods and adjust the sweetener. If you don't live near a large health food supermarket, it may be difficult to get some of these items.

You can try Amazon. If you think you will be ordering a lot from them, you might want to consider joining their Prime Pantry membership. If you are a member you will only pay $5.99 for delivery of 45 pounds or 4 cubic feet of product. Most retailers will deliver for free if you order a large amount of product, but that is only for their products. If you need to order lots of different items from several vendors, then Amazon Prime Pantry may be the way to go. Make sure you read the reviews so you have a sense of what you are getting. Remember, try to avoid ordering anything in plastic lined cans, if you can. If it doesn't say BPA free cans, then there is BPA in the lining of the cans. Since you will be mostly cooking from scratch, it will be rare that you will need anything in a can, so you don't need to stress over this unless you are eating a lot of foods from cans, like beans. Kombucha

(Chapter Six) helps rid your system of plastic and heavy metals, so make sure you are drinking it as our food and water may contain both.

Gluten Free

All recipes are gluten free. There is even a chapter on gluten free baking to introduce you to how good cakes and cookies can taste without being made of wheat flour. In Chapter Nineteen, the "Let's Bake" chapter, you will use organic sprouted brown rice flour combined with sorghum flour, instead of wheat flour for baked goods. Sorghum has a taste similar to wheat and is nutritious. It is high in protein, iron and antioxidants. However, it is somewhat coarse so it doesn't work well for pastry.

Many people have asked me why, if in the bible people lived to be over one hundred years old and ate wheat, what is the problem with wheat? The answer is that the wheat you are eating now is not the same wheat people consumed in biblical times except for Spelt. Spelt is the same wheat that was used in 5,000 B.C. Since people develop celiac disease from eating modern day wheat, which damages the lining of the small intestine, it is a really good idea to eliminate wheat, barley and rye for a week and see how you feel. According to the Celiac Support Foundation most people with celiac disease are undiagnosed. You may now be wondering, "Why not just eat Spelt?" You are welcome to do that but all gluten, which is found in wheat, barley and rye, is hard to digest and can be inflammatory.

Raw Foods

Many people swear by raw food diets because of how good they feel. Since heat does kill some of your vitamins and enzymes, raw foods have more nutrition and are very alkaline. Eating raw foods also ensure that you eliminate waste because they are so high in fiber. If you have health issues, need to lose weight or suffer from constipation, it is a good idea to eat more raw foods. However you need to make sure they are organic as fruits and vegetables have a lot of water and you don't want that water filled with chemicals. This is really important if you want to do a juice fast, otherwise you will take in a large concentration of pesticides. I am not talking about a lettuce and tomato salad when we are talking about raw foods. What I am referring to is a lettuce, spinach, kale, sunflower seed, etc. salad. If you don't like to eat salads, then consider buying the "Magic Bullet." (@$60) and juice your raw foods. The "Bullet" keeps the roughage in while a juicer takes it out. Add in pineapple, apple, carrots, etc. for flavor. Fruits and vegetables are more expensive than grains, so it will raise your budget, but it could be well worth it.

Salt

Table salt has been called a poison by many food advocates because it is somewhat toxic. The solution is simple. Use mineral rich Celtic salt or Himalayan pink salt. If you over salt your food, it may be because your body is craving something it needs. No matter what the reason, use salt in moderation. Excessive salt is hard on your kidneys and dehydrates you which is not healthy.

Caffeine

In small quantities, coffee does have some positive benefits such as stimulating the liver. However, in addition to dehydrating one, caffeine leaches the minerals out of your bones as does sugar. It affects iron absorption and your kidneys ability to retain calcium, zinc, magnesium and other important minerals. (4.5) This contributes to osteoporosis. Many nutritionists will tell you that the worst part of coffee is not necessarily the caffeine. Coffee is the most sprayed agriculture product in the world which makes it very toxic. Coffee is also very acid. You can cut down the acid by 67% if you use the "cold brew" method which is at the end of this section. The problem with trying to cut down your caffeine intake by drinking decaffeinated beverages is that the chemicals that are used to decaffeinate tea and coffee are far worse than drinking caffeine, unless you get "water processed." Arbor Teas uses the carbon dioxide method to decaffeinate their tea which is the safest. Carbon Dioxide (CO_2) decaffeinated tea is essentially "pressure cooked" with this naturally occurring gas. At high pressures and high temperatures, carbon dioxide reaches a supercritical state. The CO_2 becomes a solvent with its small, nonpolar molecules attracting the small caffeine molecules. Since flavor molecules are larger, they remain intact which is why this process best retains the flavor of the tea.

Take down your caffeine consumption slowly. Calculate how many cups of coffee/tea you are currently drinking and take it down one cup a week until you are drinking no more than two cups a day or 2 tablespoons. It is easy to cheat with this as some brands of coffee have a much higher percentage of caffeine than other brands. Start on the weekend, so by the time Monday hits you are starting to get use to the one cup less. Kombucha is weak tea, so count it as ¼ of a cup of coffee.

One of the reasons why it is so hard to kick the caffeine habit is that people do not sleep well. You may be one of those people who claim that you can drink coffee and sleep. You may be sleeping but you are not in the deep, REM sleep you need and your body is suffering. Don't drink caffeine after 2 P.M. Try the Yoga posture of "Legs up the Wall" for at least 10 minutes before you go to sleep. (You will sleep like the dead if you do this.) If you take calcium, take it before you go to sleep. I keep mine next to my toothbrush, so I can take it right after I brush my teeth at night. It will be easier to kick the caffeine habit when you are getting more rest. Studies show that lack of sleep may also contribute to weight gain. (4.6) So does living on adrenaline from drinking caffeine.

To help you cut down on your coffee consumption, following is a great recipe for Pumpkin Pie Spice Chai tea. Tea has less caffeine than coffee and green tea is alkaline, while coffee is very acid. Many families in India have their favorite Chai Tea recipe that has been handed down for generations. You are about to continue this tradition by determining what recipe works best for you. You will make enough for a week and then put in a mason jar or the like, so all you have to do is take a minute to heat it up in the morning. This recipe makes six cups of tea. When you add the milk, the total is eight to nine cups of tea. The health benefits of each ingredient are numerous. If you look each one up, you will never go a day without drinking chai again given what it does for your body. We have put in parenthesis the main benefits. Child labor is used in the tea and sugar industry, so make sure you are using "Fair Trade" tea and sugar.

This Chai Tea recipe will cost you @ 15 cents a cup. Add spices, bring your water to a boil. Turn the heat off and add tea and sweetener. Let steep for 20 minutes. If you are using loose tea, pour

Organic Chai Tea Ingredients

6 Fair Trade cardamom pods. (antioxidant) Open them up, toss the pods and crush the seeds.

1 inch, fresh organic ginger. (anti-inflammatory)

Pinch of Fair Trade Cayenne pepper. (purifies the blood)

1 tsp Fair Trade cinnamon. (manages blood sugar)

3 shakes of Fair Trade nutmeg. (reverses aging)

4 Fair Trade cloves that have been broken up. (antibacterial)

4 tsp organic, Fair Trade tea.

3 cups water.

¼ tsp stevia and 2 TB spoons organic, Fair Trade sugar.

through a strainer into a mason jar or other vessel that has a lid. It can be hot, but not so hot that it breaks your jar. Fill the pot back up with 1.5 cups water and put through the strainer again. Then fill up the pot again with another 1.5 cups water and pour into your container so you get all the tea from the leaves out. Now the fun begins! Pour a little into a cup, add the amount of milk or cream you usually drink with your tea and taste it.   If you want more cinnamon, add it. If tea is too weak, then steep some more tea. If too strong, add water. If you like the taste of cardamom, then use 8 pods next time.   If you want it spicier, add more pepper and ginger. However, if you make it too spicy it might make you feel a little nauseous if you drink spicy tea on an empty stomach. If you want your tea to taste like "Starbucks" then you need to use cream and @2-4 TB of sugar per cup, depending on the size of your cup. Look up Chai Tea recipes and experiment so that one time, you try "allspice" in

stead of cardamom or try adding anise. Try cream, almond milk or organic soy milk. Add more sweetener if you like. Perfect your "family recipe!" The tea will keep for a week. Just heat it up in the morning and add your milk. Don't store the milk in your jar as the stored milk can sour your tea. If you notice in the picture the tea in the pitcher is darker than the glass. That is because you should wait to add the milk until you are ready to serve. Best not to store your tea in a plastic container otherwise your tea will start to taste like plastic.

If you are a major coffee drinker, then make "dirty" chai. If you add coffee to your mason jar, then your tea will become acid. So what I recommend you do is put ¾ cup of tea in your pot in the morning and add 1 teaspoon of coffee with ¼ cup water and heat it up or make cold brew coffee and add. Add the milk before taking the tea off the stove and strain the coffee out. "Dirty Chai" is delicious. After drinking it for a few days, regular coffee will seem so bland. "Dirty Chai" is less acidic then regular coffee. Chai tea and dirty chai are great as iced teas. If you must have coffee, then try Cold Brew Coffee as it is 67% less acidic than regular coffee. *(4.7)* The acid in coffee can erode tooth enamel and create other health problems. To make your cold brew coffee, put the coffee in the nut bag and add the water or forget the nut bag and filter out the grounds at the end using a metal strainer. This coffee will last for two weeks without going stale, so put in the fridge and heat it up when you need it or use it for ice coffee. If not strong enough, you can add more coffee. If you only have a glass jar, then put one cup of coffee in the jar and fill to the top with water. Use as a coffee concentrate and add water when you heat it up. You will love this coffee!!

Cold Brew Coffee
1 Nut Milk Bag
Or
fine metal strainer
1 cup coffee
8 cups water
Put in fridge for 11 hours

References: (4.1) www.nomeatathlete.com/vegetarian-protein-primer "Protein—A Primer for Vegetarians, "by Matt Frazier

(4.2)   www.whfoods.com/genpage.php?tname=foodspice&dbid=84   "The World's Healthiest Foods."

(4.3) Here is the study. http://www.mdpi.com/1099-4300/15/4/1416

(4.4) New York Times. "That Tap Water Is Legal but May Be Unhealthy" By Charles Duhigg 12.16.09

(4.5) www.healthambition.com/negative-effects-of-coffee/ "7 Negative Effects of Coffee" by Jim Dillan 5.4.13

(4.6) Web MD "Sleep and Weight Gain." By Denise Mann

(4.7) The Daily Beast. "Coffee's Dirty Little Secret" Michael Meyer 8.18.09

CHAPTER FIVE

Exercise and Losing Weight

Exercise

The lymphatic system moves lymph through the body which is a clear fluid that rids the body of toxins, dead cells, fat and viruses. However your lymphatic system does not have a pump. (5.1) What this means is that unless you exercise, the toxins in your body will just sit in your lymphatic system making you feel sluggish and weakening your immune system. A weak immune system makes one vulnerable to getting all kinds of diseases. You won't stay with an exercise program unless you like it. People are motivated by pleasure and avoid pain. It is more fun to be motivated by pleasure. So if you like to dance, get a dance tape and dance! If you like to be outdoors then walk, jog or run and listen to upbeat music. If you like to read and there a gym near where you work, then go sit on the bike at lunch for 20 minutes and read. If you like to watch TV, then get a skier and watch TV while you are on it. A mini trampoline can be fun to jog on if that is what you like and for very little effort, the bouncing pumps your lymphatic system.

Natural light, first thing in the morning stimulates your hypothalamus which positively affects your mood and hormone balance. (5.2) Sunlight is also a source of Vitamin D. Too many people go from their house to their car to their job and then back home to their house and never get in any kind of natural light. You need natural light for a few minutes every day. So wake up 15 minutes early, drink your Chai Tea or Kombucha and take a 15 minute brisk walk in the morning. I pray while I walk and take my phone so when I think of something I need to do, I can talk into the microphone app on my "color notes." By the time I come back I am alert, energized, organized and ready to start my day. If you can't get out in the morning, then take a 10 to 15 minute walk at lunch or after work.

What about sunscreen you ask? Well sunscreen and sunglasses blocks the body's ability to produce vitamin D. (5.3) However, overexposure to sunlight begins to break down Vitamin D. Typical sunscreens are full of parabens, which have been linked to cancer (5.4) but a sunburn can also cause cancer. So I compromise. To make sure I get my Vitamin D, I don't use sunscreen other than some coconut oil on my face, for my 15 minute walk in the morning as the sun's rays are less intense at that time which makes it a good time to walk. I avoid afternoon sun, but if I need to be out in it for more than 15 minutes, I do use sunscreen. If you are a gardener or have another job that puts you in the sun a lot, you will need to find organic, non-nano zinc sunscreen to avoid the cancer risks for sunscreen. You can save money by ordering non-nano zinc online and making your own sunscreen. Don't use sun screens that are sprays as accidentally inhaling the ingredients in any sunscreen can cause health problems.

Yoga

Many yoga studios offer a free week of lessons. You can take advantage of that offer and take two to three classes a day. This is a great way to use some of your vacation time. When you are home, look up some of the poses you learned and create your own flow. It is important to concentrate on your breathing and posture, while doing yoga. However for many people yoga is boring, so if you need to have the TV on while you practice, better to do that than not do any yoga at all. It is important in yoga that you do it correctly or you can hurt yourself or get no benefit. You will only learn to do it correctly from a teacher who can help you. So sit in the front so the teacher can see you and continue to take classes from time to time, to make sure you haven't started slumping in your poses. Little things like making sure your knee never goes past your ankle in a lunge or warrior pose is important or you can damage your knee. If you are new to Yoga and out of shape, focus on "Restorative Yoga" "Yin Yoga," "Chair Supported Yoga Poses" and "Yoga with Props." You can use these names as search terms on the internet. There are many yoga videos to help you with your practice, but ultimately you really need a good teacher to get the most benefit from yoga.

Crawling

A great stress reducing exercise is crawling. Crawling strengthen the connectors between the right and left side of the brain, because you are using the right and left side of the body at the same time. Many therapists are incorporating crawling as part of their practice to counteract the effects of stress on the brain. So put your knee pads on and start crawling! You can accomplish the same strength building brain connector function by fast walking and pumping your arms opposite from your legs. In other words, right leg and left arm forward, with your right arm back. Then switch. Putting toddlers in walkers defeats the all-important brain connector development stage which is accomplished by crawling. For that reason it behooves us to follow God's plan and let our children crawl! (5.5)

Losing Weight

Calories that are empty and provide no nutritional value can cause the body to store extra energy from food as fat. Calories that are high in nutrients provide the body with the energy it needs to function properly, allowing it to burn excess energy from fat stores and help you burn off unwanted pounds. (5.6) It is also more satisfying to eat foods high in nutrition. You won't be eating foods you don't need because of "cravings." When you have been eating well for a period of time you will naturally gravitate towards more nutritional foods, because that is what your body "remembers." Most pregnant women need additional calcium so they crave ice cream. I craved lettuce. I couldn't get enough of it.

If you put a lot of different foods in front of people, they will eat more. Let's face it, we tend to eat a lot more food at those "all you can eat" bars. The point is, if you want to reduce your food intake keep your meals simple with no more than three items at any one meal, with one of those items being a vegetable dish. This book provides many balanced, one course meals that you can heat up in a hurry, but if you are overweight always include a vegetable at every meal as the fiber will fill you up with very few calories. I use to be overweight and verbally beat myself up all the time for not being able to stay on my diet. One day I realized that the reason why I couldn't stay on my diet is that I didn't like the food and I was hungry all the time. So I started including lots of fiber from whole grains and beans, which fills one up for very few calories. I didn't particularly like vegetables, so I learned to cook them until I loved them. Vegetables are high in fiber and also low in calories. By incorporating more fiber and vegetables, the pounds melted off.

Another problem with consuming "empty" calories with very little or no nutrition is that you will be hungry very shortly after a meal as this is your body's way of making sure you get what you need. When you use artificial sweeteners, your body is told that you took in sugar, but your body can't find it. The body's response is to make you hungry so you will eat the sugar that is missing. This is why a large percent of people who drink diet sodas are overweight. Stevia doesn't not have the "Starving After Effect" that artificial sweeteners have. (5.7) It is important if you are trying to lose weight that you eat low on the glycemic scale as diets high on the scale create weight gain for almost everyone.

If you are an overeater, try eating about 75% of what you normally eat and wait 15 minutes. The fiber in these meals will probably have you feel as full as your previous portions. Losing weight takes conscious thought. An activity that works every time to help people lose weight is to write down everything they eat. When I did this, I found out I was eating quite a bit more than I thought I was, especially carbs. By adjusting my carb consumption down, I felt so much better and lost weight. No, I didn't start eating more meat. I learned to make delicious meals with beans, like you will learn in this book. If beans make you gassy, then you need to learn to cook them correctly. You have to drain the soaking water off and add new water before you cook as the chemical that causes gas is in the soaking water.

So try eating healthy for a few weeks, go get some exercise and you will most likely lose some weight. As your energy increases, then you will feel more like exercising and feel even better and lose even more weight. You want to get yourself into a cycle that is moving towards your goals.

References: (5.1) www.babyboomermagazine.com Exercise and the Lymphatic System, by Robert Bresloff 1.13.14

(5.2) Thyroid.answers.com. The Function of the Hypothalamus and How It Relates to Your Thyroid

(5.3) in5d.com. Wearing Sunglasses Can Affect Your Pineal Gland 4.26.2011 and also the article from Livestrong.com Does SPF Block the Vitamin D From the Sun? By Cheryl Jones. 8. 16, 2013

(5.4) Huffington Post. " Is Your Sunscreen Causing Cancer?" By Dr. Mike Hart. 6.07.13

(5.5) Ohio Health. What's so important about crawling? By Heather Haring, OTR/L 4.1.2009

(5.6) Livestrong.com How to Metabolize Fat with Food, by Shannon Sukovaty. 8.16.13

(5.7) Mercola.com "Artificial Sweeteners Cause Greater Weight Gain than Sugar, Yet Another Study Reveals" by Dr. Mercola 12.4.12

CHAPTER SIX

Boost Your Immune System with Probiotics

After drinking Kombucha and Kefir Soda for a couple of weeks; energy drinks and regular soda should start to taste terrible. They will taste like what they are, which is sugar and chemicals. Instead of undermining your health, the probiotic drinks in this chapter will build your health. Your body is made up of both "good" and "bad" bacteria. When you have too much of the "bad" bacteria, you will not feel well. With that said, many people will drink quarts of these drinks to get themselves healthy fast. This might cause a "flare up" where the bad bacteria is getting eliminated so fast that your body gets a little overwhelmed. While flare-ups usually only last a few days, I believe in balance. One, 8 ounce glasses of one or the other of these drinks is sufficient to feed your intestinal flora. Kombucha can feed Candida, so if you have this issue then reduce your Kombucha intake to 4 ounces a day.

In addition to being a probiotic and helping you absorb the nutrition from your food, Kombucha has B vitamins, amino acids, vitamin C and helps your body get rid of plastic and metals. Fans of this drink swear that it improves their mood, energy levels and helps with joint function and ligament health. If you develop a passion for making probiotic drinks, then try Julia Miller's book "Delicious Probiotic Drinks" and you can try making Kvass, Kanji, Rejuvelac, etc. Since Kombucha leaches plastic and metals out of your body, you can't use any equipment that is metal or plastic when you make it or the plastic and metal will go into your drink. Don't be tempted to buy a glass mason jar with a spout as the spout is metal and could leak into your drink. You need a jar that you can lock down. You will also need water bottles to pour the Kombucha or Kefir soda into, so you can serve it. It is awkward to try and pour liquid from a large mason jar into a glass. Once you have transferred your Kombucha or Kefit soda to your "water" bottles, you can start a new batch with your original 3.5 quart mason jars so you have a continuous supply. The Container Store has beautiful 34 ounce Giara

Water Bottles in colors that will give your table a festive look.

Chlorine and pesticides kill both the Kefir Crystals and Kombucha Scoby. If you are using tap water, you will need to boil the chlorine out. Do not boil your water in Teflon. You can purchase a stainless steel "pasta" pot for very little money. You will need to buy organic sugar or the pesticides in the sugar can kill your Kefir crystals or your Kombucha Scoby. Please use Fair Trade sugar to do your part to eliminate child and slave labor in the sugar industry. Wholesome Sweeteners, which is Fair Trade and organic sells their sugar in 5 and 10 pound bags for $2 a pound at Amazon. Before you begin, wash everything with hot soapy water and rinse well to make sure you aren't growing residual bacteria from your containers.

Non Dairy Kefir Soda

Equipment & Ingredients for Kefir Soda

1- 3.5 quart mason jars,

Wooden Spoon

1/3 cup organic, fair trade sugar

1/4 tsp molasses (optional, but adds minerals)

1/8 tsp baking soda

1 quart spring water or reverse osmosis water with a pinch of pink salt added back in for minerals.

Small glass mason jar to store crystals.

1 water bottle to serve from.

1 cup Kefir Crystals. You can buy online at places like Amazon. They are sold dry and 1 TB dry makes @3 TB wet. 16 TB makes 1 cup. If you keep the crystals in sugar water in a warm place, they will grow.

Dissolve the sugar and molasses in your water. Add the crystals. Cover with a cloth napkin or cheesecloth and secure with a rubber band. (Keeps the bugs out and allows air into the mix.) After 48 hours, strain the crystals out. Then lock down the top so it carbonates for 24 hours. If not fizzy enough, then lock down for another 12 hours. Add 1 cup organic fruit or 1 cup fruit juice and lock down and put in the refrigerator overnight or for a few hours. Strain out the fruit and use it for a smoothie. Pour the soda in your water bottle and start another batch.

Don't forget about your drink when in the carbonation stage or your jars can explode after a few days. Store the crystals in a separate jar with a little sugar in the fridge. The cold has them go dormant. If you are not going to use the crystals for awhile, then add 1/2 tsp sugar per week. If the crystals start starving, they will break up and die.

Experiment with flavors. You can add lemon juice and a little sugar for lemonade without doing the carbonation step. Try adding vanilla for vanilla soda. "Wellness Mama" suggests adding raisins or prune juice and it will taste like Dr. Pepper. My favorite is Watermelon or Pineapple/Strawberry. Both fruits are sweet, so if you are using fruit that is not so sweet, you may need more fruit or add a teaspoon of sugar. You can find other suggestions online for different flavored drinks.

Kombucha

Equipment & Ingredients for Kombucha

1- 3.5 quart mason jar

Wooden Spoon

1 cup organic sugar

4 organic tea bags

Cloth/cheese cloth and rubber band to cover

3 quarts spring or reverse osmosis water with

a pinch of pink salt added back in for minerals

Kombucha Scoby, can buy online

1 glass water bottle to serve from

In the picture above is a mason jar with fruit for the last stage of the process. The scoby is on the plate. The colored water bottles make for a beautiful presentation when you serve. Making Kombucha follows a similar process as the Kefir Soda, only you will be boiling the water with the sugar. Bring sugar and water to a boil, turn off the heat and add 4 organic, tea bags. Take the tea bags out after 20 minutes. Let cool down to room temperature, pour in the mason jar and add the scoby. Cover with the cloth napkin or cheesecloth and secure with the rubber band. Wait 7 days to taste. Your Kombucha tea should be starting to taste like apple cider. If tart, it is ready. If still sweet, it needs a couple more days. If it is starting to taste like vinegar, then your house is really warm. You can add some sugar before you move to the carbonation stage. 1 teaspoon is usually enough. The vinegar taste means the Scoby has eaten all the sugar and in the carbonation stage, the live bacteria in your drink will need a tiny bit more sugar. If the Kombucha is barely sweet, you have enough sugar for the carbonation stage. Once the drink becomes tart but slightly sweet, take out the Scoby and place in another small glass mason jar with some tea to store it. Lock down the lid on your "tea" and let it carbonate for 1 to 2 days. Then add 1 cup fruit. My all-time favorite is 1/2 cup pineapple with ½ cup strawberries. You need a sweet fruit. Let the fruit sit in the drink overnight. Then strain it out and pour the drink into your water bottles and start a new batch.

If you are not going to re-use the Scoby right away, then pour 1 cup of tea over it and put it away for future use. Check on it in four days to see if the jar needs to be "burped" so it doesn't explode. Once the Scoby has eaten all the sugar, it stops carbonating so you can store like this for a week. If you want to store longer, in order to keep the Scoby from dying you will need to add 1 tsp of sugar and burp it every couple of days. When you are ready to make your next batch, add the 1 cup Kombucha tea that you stored the Scoby in. By adding the Kombucha tea that is already fermented, your new batch of tea will be ready two days sooner. So if the last batch took seven days, the new batch will take five days.

Fermented Vegetables

People ask me all the time, how they can get rid of the pesticides in their body. Fasting is one way, but often overwhelms the body and can make people sick. I would recommend eating foods with healthy bacteria in them which supports the body in detoxifying. Eating foods without pesticides will also help the body detoxify. So will exercise. Once you have given your body a chance to detoxify normally, then you might want to consider doing a doctor supervised juice fast.

Cultured Foods for Life tells us that one of the best bacteria to use to get rid of pesticides is Lactobacillus Plantarum, which you will find in cultured/pickled vegetables. Not only does it help the body get rid of pesticides, it also helps control Candida and many other ills like irritable bowel syndrome. Fermented vegetables also help digest your food. You can get more recipes than what we have here at the "Cultured Foods" website. (www.culturedfoodlife.com) Try and get into the habit of eating some cultured vegetables at each meal. My favorite is Kimchi. Here is a simple recipe for Korean pickled cabbage (Kimchee) that I love to eat with any meal, mixing it into my rice.

Kim Chee

Ingredients and Equipment

1 glass 3 quart mason jar

1 Head of Chinese Cabbage

1/4 cup sea salt

3 inch piece of ginger

½ tsp sugar

4 to 6 cloves of garlic

1 to 2 tsp of Korean or cayenne pepper

Optional: scallions, peppers, radish, etc.

Kim Chee Directions

If you don't like spicy food, then use ½ tsp or a dash of the chili pepper. What you want is the bacteria from this fermented vegetable and the spice is not necessary to make the bacteria. You can also add 2 to 4 cups of other vegetables like carrot, turnip, cucumber, etc. shredded or chopped small. Sprinkle the salt on the cabbage and put in a bowl with a plate on top and a weight on top of the plate. Leave at room temperature for 4 hours. Rinse the salt off. In a glass jar add 4 cups water and 1 TB salt, the garlic and ginger. Peel the ginger first. Put in a cupboard for 7 to 10 days. Take it out and taste it. Does it taste similar to a spicy sauerkraut? If so, then it is ready to put in the refrigerator for 6 to 8 weeks so it can "cure." Use a small amount (2 TB) with your meals. In addition to adding good bacteria and spice, Kimchee helps you digest your meal. As with everything, you want to eat in moderation so you don't overdue your salt. Best if you have 1 - 3.5 quart jar and 1 - 1 quart jar. When you have 1 quart left of the pickled cabbage, then transfer to the 1 quart jar and start a new batch.

If an opaque white film appears at the top during the 1 week fermentation process, that is okay. However no other color should appear. If you see black or dark brown, toss everything as you now have mold in your pickles. Listen to your body always. If you don't feel well after eating anything, then don't eat it again. Toss it. You don't know what may have been put in your food or if you accidentally cross contaminated your food because you used a utensil that had bacteria on it when you made any of these probiotic drinks and pickles.

5 Minute Cold Start Yogurt	Budget
6 oz container of organic yogurt	$2.00
2 TB organic powdered milk	.50
1 quart of organic grass fed milk (32 oz)	2.50
$3.00 divided by 6, 6 ounce jars is 50 cents.	

Cold Start Yogurt Directions

If you love yogurt, then purchase a yogurt maker and make your own. Just mix the milk, 2 TB of powdered organic milk and the yogurt in a container. If you use a wisk, it goes faster. Pour in the six glass jars in your yogurt maker and plug it in. Eight hours makes a thin yogurt. Ten hours is thicker but more sour. The difference between Kefir and Yogurt is how thick the yogurt is. If you want a "Greek" yogurt consistency, you will need to strain your yogurt through cheesecloth. Make sure your hands and utensils are all very clean, having been washed in hot soapy water. You are growing bacte-ria and you don't want to grow residual bacteria that was in one of your containers or on your hands. Save 6 ounces of yogurt for the next batch which will save you the $2.00 for the starter and bring your costs down to 50 cents a jar. If you have a larger yogurt maker, then you need to save 6 ounces of yo-gurt for every 32 oz of milk that you use.

If your body hurts, you will need to give up dairy as dairy is both acidic and inflammatory. If you are healthy, then you are welcome to include it in your diet from time to time like we have in this book. If you are eating dairy every day, then try to develop habits where you are consuming it a lot less often. I use organic, grass fed milk which is the highest quality milk in terms of nutrition. It is hard to find grass fed organic yogurt and if you could, you would most likely pay at least $2 (or more) for 6 ounces. That doesn't make sense when you can make it yourself for 50 cents for 6 ounces in less than 5 minutes and then just let it sit overnight in a yogurt maker. There is a crock pot version of yogurt that you can find on the web that is a little complicated. I prefer the cold start method because it takes 5 minutes. Every time a recipe calls for mayonnaise, you can use yogurt for lower fat content and higher protein.

CHAPTER SEVEN

Let's Get Started

Chapters Nine through Fifteen provide seven sessions of how to make three meals in one hour or a leisurely one and half hours, sipping wine, etc. while you cook. You will eat each meal twice in one week, so the total is six meals. By following the instructions for those six chapters, you will learn to intuitively cook in a way that is efficient and balanced without taking a lot of time. Many of you are overwhelmed at this point? Where do you start, you ask? Simple, just ask yourself what is your worst habit? Do you drink soda, then go to Chapter Six and go online and order your Scoby and Kefir crystals and learn how to make extremely healthy drinks that you love. Are you a candy eater? If a "sweet tooth" is your weakness, then go to Chapter Nineteen and learn to bake deserts or Chapter Twenty for Chocolate Lovers and wean yourself off candy which is often made from GMO corn syrup and artificial flavoring and color. In the beginning you are welcome to just purchase organic gluten free baking mix to keep things simple. If you bake a lot it is a good idea to make your own "Baking Mix" to save money. At the end of Chapter Eight is a recipe for a baking mix that is superior to what you can purchase in a store. Are you out in the sun every day, then go to Chapter Twenty One and order the products you need to make organic sunscreen. Do you drink more than one cup of coffee a day? Then buy Fair Trade organic coffee this week and make cold brew coffee to cut down on your acid intake. Better yet, make Chai tea or "Dirty Chai" with alkaline green tea to make your diet more alkaline.

Take your time. Start substituting a few meals a week from the recipes and keep eating how you normally do. I know many of you do not know how to cook. We now have a whole generation of people in their 20's and 30's who don't know how to cook because their mothers worked and they didn't have time to show them. Take heart, I have made this simple. If you don't know how to cook, then allow twice the recommended time at first until you get the rhythm of how cooking flows. Just add a couple new food items a week until almost your entire diet is healthy and balanced. I say " almost," because everyone needs to eat out from time to time. So what do I grab when I am "out and about" and starving? I choose a bean and cheese burrito in a flour tortilla from a fast food drive

through.   All the toxins in corn tortillas and hormones in meat make me kind of sick to think about it so I avoid those foods. I can handle the tiny bit of hormones I will get from the cheese and pesticides from the beans and tortilla because this is a once a week occurrence. I usually pack water, a peanut butter sandwich and an apple when I am out and about.

Over six chapters, you will be cooking main courses like chili, casseroles, meat loaf, shepherd's pie, sushi, etc. Recipes are simple. If you would like to make them more complicated, please feel free but it will take you more time.   If you are a "snack" eater then go to Chapter Eighteen and make up some healthy ones you can just grab.   The plan is to cook from scratch for an hour once a week. So start thinking how you will make this hour fun.   Drink some wine and/or put on a sports game to watch while you cook or pull up your favorite TV program on your laptop and bring it into the kitchen.

This program is designed for the working professional or working parents, who have little time to cook during the week.   This program will not only save you the money from eating out, it will also save you a lot of time as even eating "fast" food requires that you wait in a line to get it. Having balanced, healthy food available that you can just heat up and create a meal takes planning. Have you ever come home and looked in the refrigerator and there was nothing to eat?!   If you are going to eat healthy, you need to always have your refrigerator filled with food that you can just heat up because very few people come home from work and want to cook a meal. Instead of pulling out some processed food that you heat up that is full of pesticides and empty of nutrition, you will pull out your pre-prepared meals. Yes, you will be eating left overs like casseroles.   However the kind of food you will be creating will actually taste as good as the first time you made it or better the next day.

For example, if you have spaghetti sauce already made up, you can put together a pizza in 5 minutes or lasagna in 15 or simply cook noodles and make a salad for a spaghetti dinner. If you like to barbecue, you can cook your chicken in the oven for half an hour one evening or Saturday, while you are cooking your casseroles. Then cool and put in a glass container in the fridge. This will cut your barbecue time by 70%. Then sometime in the next three days, you can cook on the barbecue for 10 minutes with sauce. It tastes great, just try it.   While you are barbecuing, you can heat up some Spanish rice or mashed potatoes that you made in advance and quickly steam some vegetables.

Another idea along this line that is gaining popularity is "Mason Jar Salads." By layering the vegetables, dressing and lettuce in a specific order, the lettuce does not get soggy.   You can make up in advance, as many as you can eat in five days. Make up some cornbread or Quinoa muffins and you will have a light meal that you can just grab out of your refrigerator.   Just google "Mason Jar Salads" to get ideas and find the layering directions.

My freezer always has several containers of frozen beans, sauces and frozen meat.   If I am out of food, then when I get up in the morning I take out some cream of chicken soup and a chicken breast from the freezer and put it in the fridge. If I don't have rice, then I start soaking some in the rice cooker and start cooking it as soon as I get home. While the rice is cooking, I start cutting up the chicken for the chicken broccoli casserole that I can have ready in less than 15 minutes. Soaked rice only takes @15 minutes to cook. All I need to do is sauté half a diced onion with the cut up chicken breast for 5 minutes, add in some broccoli and half a cup of water and steam together for 5 minutes. Then mix in with the rice and cream of chicken soup and add in 1/3 cup of parmesan cheese and broil for 3 minutes. I always make enough for two meals, so in 15 minutes (5 minutes to cut up the onion and chicken) I have one meal and another for the next day that takes 5 minutes to heat up.

Or you can do the above scenario in reverse if you want a lunch to take to work. Just take out what you need the night before like Alfredo or spaghetti sauce. Then in the morning you can cook the noodles while you get dressed. Then put the noodles and sauce together and take it to work.   I often use a double boiler and cook the noodles in the lower half and steam a vegetable in the top half. The point is that by rotating from my freezer to my refrigerator, I can manage everything so I always have high quality meals available.

Tasting Your Food

You won't eat the food unless you like it.   For that reason, in every recipe there will be instructions to taste it with recommendations on how to change the taste if it is too bland, etc.   No matter how good your intentions, you won't eat healthy food if you do not like it. You will start dreaming of your favorite junk food and you will find yourself binging.

I am a salty, spicy type so I add cayenne pepper to everything, including Chai Tea. I think sweet pickles and candy is sickenly sweet. If you are the opposite, then if you are using alkaline flours for baking like millet or quinoa which tend to be bitter, then add a teaspoon of sugar. If the curry/yogurt/lentil soup tastes too bland, add a little sugar as many commercial curry recipes have corn syrup or sugar or a similar ingredient. If your baked goods like pancakes are too bland, then add some fat in the form of oil. Too wet, use less liquid next time. Almost all commercial foods have a lot of salt, sugar and msg in them so your taste buds want that taste. If you savor your food, one thing you will probably notice with organic and whole foods is that they have a lot more flavor so you will need less salt, etc. You need to experiment until your food tastes the way you like it. With each dish take a little out and try seasoning it in different ways. Find a combination that works, then season the entire dish. I recommend that you start by making the dishes in small quantities to see if you like it. After a few weeks you will have a menu of foods you really like with a kitchen stocked with the raw ingredients you need to "cook on a whim."

If your idea of a great meal is a one pound steak with a potato and a lettuce and tomato salad dripping in GMO salad dressing, then try a ¾ pound of steak, keep your potato and learn how to make a vegetable dish that you like. While not completely acid/alkaline balanced, that meal will be so much healthier than what you have been eating. Best to make small changes or you could get discouraged with the whole idea of trying to eat healthier. With regard to tasting your food, never, ever taste raw eggs or meat. You will be instructed to taste the dish before you add the eggs or meat. One mother and daughter that I know wound up in the hospital after making chocolate chip cookies because they kept tasting the raw cookie dough which had eggs in it.

Food Safety

Always wash your hands. If one of your dishes will be raw like a salad, make it first and then handle your meat. If that is not possible, then always wash your hands after you have handled meat or eggs before you handle any other food item. Honestly, I wouldn't handle raw meat and then make a salad. If you just handled raw meat and want a vegetable, then make a steamed vegetable instead. We now have anti-biotic resistant salmonella in foods that is only killed through heat. Make sure you have two small breadboards for cutting. One is for meat, the other is for potatoes, fruits and vegetables. Do not let the two cutting surfaces touch when you store them. Bacteria from meat can live in the cutting cracks. When you are done with the boards, wash them in the dishwasher. If any of your vegetables or fruits have mold on them, wash your board with hot soapy water before you cut anything else on it. NEVER, EVER cut up your fruits and vegetables on a board that was just used for meat. If you don't have another board, then put parchment paper down on a counter or a clean towel and cut on that.

Eating at Work/ Time Savers for Busy Professionals

Okay, so you work over 60 hours a week as a "professional" which means you probably don't care as much about the money as much as you care about the time it takes to prepare meals and eat. So make three portions for each dish you cook. Put in glass containers in your freezer and put in the fridge when you leave in the morning for dinner or take to work. I was in that category, so I cooked and prepared foods for 1.5 hours on the weekend and made enough food for myself and my children to last the entire week. One hour was for cooking the meals and another half hour to make up the Kombucha and other items I needed. All I had to do after that was heat up everything when I got home. I also kept a lot of food at my job, so I didn't eat garbage from the machines when I had to work late. While people half my age got the flu and every other virus that came along, I worked through the winter without ever getting sick.

I recommended that you get a toaster oven for your job, so you can have a hot meal at work. So plan out what scenario you need for the lifestyle you are living and write out a flow chart for the week so you know what you will need. We will include a descrip-tion of how the week will flow for the first few cooking chapters. After doing this for a few weeks, you won't need the meal planning instructions anymore. You will naturally plan for the next couple of days so it all works for you.

Presentation

Throughout the book are pictures of meals being served that are acid/alkaline balanced and low on the glycemic index. The pictures demonstrate to new cooks or busy people that with a few place-mats and half a dozen different dishes, you can create festive and attractive meals. You can use black rice to make a statement and there are so many different colors among vegetables and fruits, it is easy to create an attractive meal with very little effort. This book is for people who need to get food on the table for their family and need simple ideas for presentations that are realistic for a busy schedule. For those of you that have talent and enjoy creating beautiful scenes with your food, knock yourself out. It is part of the joy of cooking and the food will taste better, I promise. If you family is concerned that you might be feeding them "health food," an attractive presentation will often ally their fears. I pick the flowers when I am out on my walk in the morning and put in some water, for use later. You don't need to purchase flowers. With a few simple items that are local, you can create an imaginative and beautiful table.

CHAPTER EIGHT

Routine For The Week

Preparing Grains and Beans to Eat

Every week, you will prepare the grains and beans you need for the week in advance. This will save you an enormous amount of time and make it possible to come home and put together a meal in less than 15 minutes. Grains and beans contain phytic acid which blocks the absorption of minerals. The outer shell has the most phytic acid which means that bran is a disaster. Grains and beans also contain enzyme inhibitors that interfere with the absorption of protein. U.S. grown grains also contain arsenic. It is for that reason that many books will advise you not to eat grains as the acids and enzymes obviously will create a break down in your health, However some of the healthiest people on the planet eat a diet rich in grains and beans and reducing the arsenic, phytic acid and enzyme inhibitors is easy. You can purchase "organic, sprouted brown rice" or simply soak your grains and beans for at least 7 hours before you cook them. Many cultures know to soak their grains before cooking. If you are concerned about arsenic, then boil your rice in six times the water, instead of using a rice cooker. When cooked, drain off the excess water and let sit with the top off so the excess water steams out. Not only do you remove most of the phytic acid and aresenic by soaking, it begins to sprout the rice. Sprouted rice is far more nutritious than regular rice containing four times the vitamin E of regular rice and three times the B vitamins (8.1) and it tastes so much better. "To Your Health" sells both organic sprouted brown rice and organic sprouted brown rice flour at $4 a pound if your purchase the 10 Pound bag at Amazon. That is $1.50 a pound cooked. If you eat baked goods like pancakes more than once a week, you really should consider making up your own baking mix using organic sprouted brown rice flour. The recipe is at the end of this chapter.

If you are doing the soaking method, then start soaking your grains or beans before you go to work or before you go to sleep at night. Then pour off the soaking water and then add the water needed to cook in your rice cooker. For beans, best to cook all day or overnight in a crock pot so you don't have to watch it. Add 4 cups of water for each cup of beans. Pouring off the soaking water also prevents gas. The actual amount of time this will take you is @ 6 minutes to put the rice in a bowl, soak, pour off the water, refill and push the button to start the rice or beans. Cook WITHOUT salt.

Yes, I know you can buy organic beans for $1.25 for a 15 oz can. However I can tell you from personal experience that I get gas from canned beans and I don't from the beans I cook myself, so I question if they were prepared correctly. The savings to make the beans yourself is not that significant but what is significant is the fact that you know they were prepared correctly and you aren't using beans from plastic lined cans. If you don't have a crock pot, then use 5 times the water to beans ratio and bring to a boil and turn down to simmer for an hour. When done, drain before you store them.

Crock pots and rice cookers will keep you from burning food or burning the house down. Just make sure they are made from stainless steel and not aluminum or Teflon. Beans freeze well so make four batches and put three in glass containers in the freezer. This way, I only cook beans once a month. Personally I don't like the taste of frozen grains, so I make a fresh batch each week. I have taught people who "couldn't boil water" to cook. When I explained what we were going to do, they always thought it sounded complicated and time consuming. Once they made some meals, they were amazed at how easy cooking can be and were encouraged to become cooks. So try not to judge until you have made a dish or tried the soaking and cooking method for rice and beans. If you are organized, it takes very little work to set yourself up to always have healthy meals. I soak my beans and rice on Friday nights, then cook on Saturday morning. If I need to make Kombucha, I also boil the tea on Friday night and then let it cool overnight and add the Scoby in the morning.

Beans

    1 cup beans

    4 cups water

    Soak for 7 hours

    Pour the water off

    Add 3 cups fresh water

Cook in a crock pot for 3 hours or longer.

Grains

    1 cup rice

    3 cups water

    Soak for 7 hours

    Pour the water off

    Add 1.5 cups water

Cook in a rice cooker. If using a pot, bring to a boil and then simmer for 20-25 minutes If your rice has absorbed a lot of the soaking water, then add 1.2 cups to cook instead of 1.5.

Snacks for the Week

Do you like potatoes and/or yams for snacks or for a side dish? Then pop some in the oven when you are making casseroles. Then you will only need 5 minutes to heat them up when you want a snack. Yes, you can cook a potato in the microwave for 5 minutes but the heat is so high, it could destroy most of the nutrition.   Cooked potatoes and yams will last for a week in the fridge and both are almost in the middle for the acid/alkaline scale, but high on the glycemic index, so only eat one for a snack. Don't like potatoes? Then go to Chapter Eighteen and make up some granola bars or try some of the other snacks like garbanzo bean dip and chips in Chapter Seventeen.

Grilled Chicken

Only one more step and you will have what you need to make up bowls, burritos and salads that are a meal. On Friday night, take out some chicken breasts. On Saturday morning, marinate 3 pounds in 2 TB vinegar, 4 TB oil, 1 tsp salt and 1 TB seasoning. You could try Italian, Mesquite, Chili and Cumin, etc. Go take your shower then cook. When done, store in a glass container in the fridge. It doesn't take long to grill chicken breasts that have been sliced ½ inch thick. If they get too dry, you can always steam. The chicken, rice and beans provide the core ingredients you need to make bowls, burritos and/or quesadillas in 5 minutes. You just need some salsa and corn for the bowls and burritos. You can also add lettuce, sour cream or avocado. Some restaurants use Teriyaki sauce for their bowls. You can find sauce recipes in Chapter Seventeen. You could even put 3 oz of chicken on a plate, add rice or a yam and a small salad or steam a vegetable and you have a meal. To make six meals with the three pounds of chicken, you will need four cups of beans and eight cups of rice. That is seven pounds of food. In my experience salsa goes bad pretty quickly, so instead of buying it all you need to do is dice up some red onion, tomatoes and cilantro and add to your bowl or burrito. Then sprinkle salt and spices like chili powder. Or you can make a bowl of salsa in a food processor.

If your rice starts getting hard, it will still work for the recipes like meat loaf and chicken casserole. For the bowls and burritos you need it fluffy. Two minutes in a steamer will fluff it right up again. My family could live on bowls and burritos and their cousin quesadillas. That might not work for you however you will need rice that is already cooked for many of the casserole recipes. If bowls and burritos are not your thing, then you will need to figure out a variation of this that you have cooked in advance like casseroles. There are several suggestions for healthy casseroles throughout the book.

In the following chapters, you will make three main dishes per chapter that you will use for six meals. You will add in another four meals with the burritos and bowls. That leaves four meals where you can make spaghetti, hamburgers, etc. In every chapter, you will be making food you can freeze like chili, stew, soup, etc. so you can just pull out in the morning and have a meal that you only need to heat up in when you get home from work. My freezer is full of frozen food so I can take a break from cooking several times a week.

Ingredients for Bowls or Burritos	Organic Budget
3 oz chicken	$1.31
2 cups rice	.50
¼ cup corn	.35
1 cup black beans	.25
¼ avocado	.35
½ tomato	.50
1 – 3 TB sour cream or sauce or salsa	.25

Total for 1.5 pound burrito or bowl is $3.50. To make a 2 pound bowl and keep your costs under $4, add more rice and beans. If you are making burritos, add 30 cents for the tortilla.

Baking Mix

From time to time, the cooking sessions will include making muffins or breads to eat with a soup or stew. By making up your baking mix is advance it only takes 5 to 10 minutes to wisk together a muffin. For now you can buy some organic, gluten free mix and if you like the muffins and breads in this book, you can purchase the raw ingredients online. So far, I haven't been able to find an organic, gluten free baking mix that uses sprouted brown rice flour. If I could, most likely it would cost me quite a bit more than what I can make it for. If you need a "nut free" baking mix, "Wholesome Chow" makes one. "Authentic Foods" has a tapioca flour that is "nut free." If you need to eat gluten free and want to get started on this, then purchase aluminum free baking powder and baking soda that is available online or in most health food stores. Most likely you will need to go to Amazon to order the flours you will need. Many of Anthony's flours are "nut free" and they don't charge shipping for their organic tapioca and potato flour for orders over $35 but they don't carry organic sprouted brown rice flour. While not "nut free" you can find the sprouted rice flour at Azure Standard and if you have a drop off point near you, you won't have to pay UPS ground shipping which can cost almost as much as the flour. You will only pay an 8.5% gas fee to the driver which comes to $1.26 for a 5 pound bag and no tax unless you live in Oregon. Company policies change, so if "nut free" is a concern, make sure you contact the company at the time you place your order. If you are concerned about bugs, then freeze your flour in an air tight container so no moisture gets in for a few hours.

Flours to purchase

4 pounds of organic sprouted brown rice flour

2 pounds of organic tapioca flour

2 pounds of organic potato flour

1 pound organic sorghum flour

1 pound of organic millet flour

Directions to Make the Baking Mix

Mix the flours well with the soda, baking powder, gum and salt. Store the baking mix and leftover flours in air tight containers in a cool cupboard.

Baking Mix Recipe

6 cups organic sprouted brown rice flour

3 cups organic tapioca flour – Adds "spring" to your baked goods.

1 cup organic potato flour or starch – Adds a more refined texture.

1 TB plus 1 tsp salt

1 TB plus 1 tsp baking soda

4 TB aluminum free baking powder

1 TB plus 1 tsp xanthan gum

Cost of Baking Mix is @$1.25 per cup

References: (8.1) Live Strong.com The Nutrition of Sprouted Brown Rice May 14, 2014 | By Sara Ipatenco

CHAPTER NINE- MAIN MEALS ONE

Meat Loaf, Soup and Stew

This week you will learn how to make a healthy meatloaf, the all American staple, stew and a filling soup with bread that will be a meal. The chapters are organized so that you will make red meat dishes one week and chicken dishes another week. This saves time. For each cooking session, please read through the entire chapter before you purchase your ingredients. This session will take 1 hour to make up three dishes for two people that will be eaten twice during the week. If you are single, then either cut the recipes in half or make only one dish at a time from these chapters. All chapters assume you have rice and beans already made up. The first time you cook it will take you longer, so keep that in mind. Even if you don't think you want to make up three different meals at once, try it. You may really like the efficiency and cooking this way ensures that you will always have a meal that you can put together in 5 minutes. You will always make enough of each dish for two meals. By adding in the meals from chapter eight, you will have enough for the week. Since the meatloaf takes the longest to cook, make that dish first. Then scroll down and make the quinoa or corn muffins as they take 25 minutes to cook. Then make the stew and then the soup. If you are new to cooking, then start with one dish and then try making two or go to Chapter Fourteen where you will learn how to make one dish and season it three different ways for three different meals. If you are confused by the directions, then make the dish a couple of times before you move on to the next dish. If you don't eat red meat, but do eat chicken, then go to the next chapter and cook those meals. For the meat loaf, vegetables without a strong taste like yellow squash, cauliflower and onions work best.

Meat/Rice Loaf Directions

Preheat oven to 350. Put your vegetables and onion in your food processor and dice. Put in a bowl with the rest of the ingredients from page 52; hamburger, rice, catsup and seasonings. If you want a dish that tastes more like meat loaf, then leave the vegetables out and cook them separately and serve on the side so that your meal is acid/alkaline balanced. Mix with your hands. Then pat down in an 8 by 8 pyrex dish and cook at 350 for 40 minutes.

Meat Loaf	Organic Budget
1 pound hamburger	$7.00
1 onion	.50
3 cups cooked brown rice	.75
2 cups assorted vegetables	2.00
¼ cup catsup	.50
2 TB Gluten Free Soy Sauce	.30
1 TB Italian Seasoning	.10
1 tsp salt	.10

Total is $11.25 divided by 4 servings is @$3.00 per serving.

Beef Stew	Organic Budget
3/4 pound of stew meat	$7.00
½ carton organic beef broth	2.00
3 small potatoes	1.50
2 cups vegetables	2.00
2 TB Soy Sauce	.50

Total is $13.00 divided by 4 servings is $3.25 per serving.

Stew Directions

To make the stew, dice an onion and begin sautéing your stew meat with the onion in a pot. *Put ½ cup aside for the soup.* In your food processor, add in the vegetables for the stew. Only pulse a couple of time as you want the vegetables in fairly large chunks. Add to your meat and onions. Cut the potatoes in large chunks, 6 pieces for a small potato. Add the potatoes to the pot. *Take out 1 cup of the beef broth and set aside for the soup.* Add the remaining beef broth to your ingredients in the stew pot. Add seasonings and cut up tomato and bring to a boil. Then simmer for 10 to 15 minutes. Taste it. If your beef broth did not have much salt in it, you will need to add some, so add slowly and taste. If you al-ready know what spices you like, then add before you simmer. If you are not sure, then take out half a cup and add a pinch of basil, a bay leaf, a pinch of oregano and a pinch of Italian seasoning. Simmer for a couple of minutes and taste. Adjust to your liking and add what works for you to the pan. You can try cumin and chili powder for more of a Latin taste. There are lots of stew recipes on the inter-net. One of my all-time favorites is a Persian stew because I like lamb and turmeric.

Soup

1 cup lentils

2 cups of diced vegetables like onions, carrots, etc.

Beef Broth

Soup Directions

Rinse the lentils and bring to a boil. Simmer for 20 minutes and add the vegetables. Divide into 2 bowls. Freeze one of the bowls for next week when you will be making chicken lentil curry soup. In the second bowl, add the remaining beef broth, ½ cup of onion/stew meat and 1 TB soy sauce and salt. When you are ready to eat, simply bring to a boil and simmer for 2 minutes. Cost is $3.50 for 2 servings.

Quinoa or Corn Bread/Muffins	Organic Budget
1.5 cup baking mix	$2.25
1 cup organic cornmeal or cooked Quinoa	1.00
2-3 eggs (2 large, 3 medium)	1.00
½ cube or ¼ cup butter	.75
¼ cup organic fair trade sugar	.25
¼ tsp Stevia	.10
1 tsp salt	.10
1 cup buttermilk (1 TB vinegar in 1 cup milk) (coconut milk)	1.20
Total is $6.65 divided by 6 servings is $1.10	

Muffin Directions

This recipe is enough for four meals and two snacks or four meals and one breakfast. Left over muffins make a great snack. Just heat up in the toaster oven and put butter or honey or jam on them. If you don't want them for a snack, then divide the recipe in half. If you don't like corn or quinoa bread, then buy or make some bread that you like or make biscuits from Chapter Nineteen and subtract the ingredients for the corn/quinoa bread from your shopping list.

Take the butter out first, cut into six pieces and let it soften while you pull out your other ingredients. Add vinegar to the milk or coconut milk and wait 5 minutes. Them beat together the eggs, butter and milk. Then add in dry ingredients and stir until moistened before beating. Add raisins, seeds, etc. if you like. Pour into muffin cups or a pyrex dish and cook at 350 for 25 minutes for muffins or 40 minutes for the pyrex dish. If you are using a stainless steel muffin pan, (best to not use Teflon), then use cup-cake paper so you don't have to deal with your muffins sticking. Check when almost done by sticking a knife in the middle. It is done when the knife comes out dry and the top is just beginning to brown. Note how long your cooking time needs to be for the next time you make this dish as every oven is slightly different. Altitude makes a difference, as does the rack you cook on.

Serving the Meals. Meals 1-9 will take you 7 minutes to heat up and be ready to serve.

Meals 1 and 5: Soup and bread

Meals 2, 6 and 9: Chicken bowls and/or burritos

Meals 3 and 7: Meat/Rice Loaf with a steamed vegetable

Meals 4 and 8: Beef Stew and Muffins.

Meals 10-14: You could make spaghetti with a salad or hamburgers or whatever meals you would normally make with red meat to create variety.

CHAPTER TEN-MAIN MEALS TWO

Chicken Casseroles and Lentil Yogurt Curry Soup

To begin, take out the frozen lentil and vegetable soup from the week before and a container of black beans. If you are starting with this chapter, you will need to cook 1 cup lentils with 3 cups water. Bring to a boil and simmer for 20 minutes. You will need six cups of cooked rice for this chapter. In case you started with this chapter, please read through the entire chapter before you purchase your ingredients. This session is an hour to make up six meals. Even if you don't think you want to make up three different meals at once, try it. All recipes are enough food for two meals for two people. The directions call for you to cook both the onion and chicken together for both dishes in one pan and then split the ingredients for each casserole. So if you are only making up one casserole, use half an onion and 1 pound of chicken. With that being said, it will only take you 15 more minutes to make the second casserole and then you will have more food for the week.

Cream of Broccoli Casserole	Organic Budget
1 pound of chicken	$7.00
3 cups of cooked brown rice	.75
1 stalk of broccoli	.50
1.4 cup Parmesan cheese	.50
½ onion	.50
1 serving Cream of Chicken Soup	.75
1 TB Italian Seasoning	Total is $10.00 divided by 4 servings is 2.50

Organic Cream of Chicken Soup

1 container of chicken broth

2 cups milk

¾ cup rice flour

You will only need 1/3 of this recipe for each casserole. Divide the rest into two containers and freeze.

Cream of Chicken Soup Directions

Take out ½ cup of the chicken broth from the whole container and set it aside for the lentil soup. Wisk together the milk, remaining broth and flour. Bring almost to a boil, stirring constantly. Divide into three. Add one third to the bowl for the broccoli casserole. You will be freezing the other two servings for when you need cream of chicken soup again.

Directions for the Broccoli Casserole

If you will be making both casseroles, sauté one onion and two pounds of chicken together. After 3 to 4 minutes, add ½ cup of water and steam until all the water has boiled out. Cut one piece of chicken in half to see if it is done. No pink should be left. Take out 1/3 cup of the chicken/onion mixture and set aside for the lentil soup. Divide the rest in half and put half in an 8/8 pyrex dish for the Mexican Casserole.

If you are only making the Broccoli Casserole and not the Mexican Casserole or lentil soup, then start here with your directions. To the sautéed chicken/onion mixture in the pan, add the diced broccoli with 1/3 cup water and steam until the broccoli is done. A fork stuck in the middle should come out easily. If not, then add a little more water and steam again. Broccoli should be crisp. While you are waiting for the chicken/broccoli mixture to cook, take a second pyrex dish and add three cups of rice, one serving of the cream of chicken soup and ¼ cup parmesan cheese in the dish. Add the chicken/onion/broccoli mixture with the Italian seasoning and mix well. Cover and put in the fridge. Since all the ingredients in this casserole are already cooked, all you need to do is heat up in a 350 degree oven for 15 minutes when you are ready to eat and add a vegetable side dish to achieve your acid/alkaline balance.

Directions to Make the Mexican Casserole

Combine the onion and chicken with the rice and the cumin and chili powder. This is your first layer. Now start layering the rest of the ingredients. Add the corn and then the black beans on top of the rice. Then add the corn chips, then the salsa on top. Lastly, add the cheese. You can cover and put in the fridge to cook when you are ready to eat. Since everything is already cooked, you only need to heat up in a 350 degree oven for 15 minutes. Serve with a vegetable side dish for your acid alkaline balance. Since this dish is somewhat dense, a salad goes well with this casserole. Experiment when you make salads and try adding whatever vegetables you may have, like broccoli, zucchini, etc.

Mexican Casserole	Organic Budget
¾ pound of chicken. Best if they are skinless chicken breasts	$5.25
3 cups of cooked brown rice (@1.25 cups raw)	.75
1/2 onion	.50
1 cup corn chips	.50
1 cup frozen corn	1.00
1 cup black beans	.35
4 oz salsa red or green	1.40
4 oz cheese	1.75
1 tsp cumin	.10
1 tsp chili powder	.10
½ tsp salt	.10
Total of @$11.80 for 4 servings or @$3.00 per serving.	

Lentil Yogurt Curry Sauce/Soup

Take the lentils/vegetables mix out of the freezer from the week before. Add the 1/3 cup of the chicken/onion mixture that you set aside, to the lentils together with ½ cup chicken broth. Put an air tight lid on it and put in the fridge. The day you serve this, you will cook all together for 5 minutes then put in a blender to make a cream like soup. Then flavor to taste. I love yogurt and curry, so for every 1.5 cups of soup, I add 2 ounces of yogurt and ¼ tsp curry powder. In India, they serve Yogurt Curry Lentil sauce over rice as pictured below. This meal is as good as any restaurant, only this meal cost you less than $3. If you don't like curry and yogurt, then just salt to taste and add Italian Seasoning. This sauce/soup freezes very well, so freeze any that you don't eat in 4 days and pull out for a great meal at another time. Serve with cornbread, quinoa muffins, biscuits or rice. This meal is acid/alkaline balanced and has plenty of protein from the lentils and chicken in the soup. Enjoy!

Serving the Meals

Meals: 1 and 5, Serve the Mexican Casserole

Meals: 2 and 6, Serve the Soup and Muffins

Meals: 3 and 9, Serve the Broccoli Casserole

Meals: 4, 7 and 10, serve the burritos or bowls.

Meals: 8, 11-14, make spaghetti etc. and/or pull out some frozen stew from the week before.

CHAPTER ELEVEN-MAIN MEALS THREE

Shepard's Pie, Chili and Latin Salad

This week, you will be making Shepard's Pie in a way that it is acid/alkaline balanced as a one course meal for lunch or just to keep things simple. The chili is often a family favorite and freezes well, so you might want to make double the recipe. If you like salad and Mexican food, you will love the salad and it is very healthy. You will need rice and black beans already made up, as well as three cups of kidney beans for the chili so cook your beans the day before you begin this session. Then each dish will take very little time to cook.

Shepard's Pie	Organic Budget
1 pound hamburger	$7.00
4 large potatoes, red or golden	1.75
4 TB butter or 1 TB butter & 2 TB cream cheese	.75
1 TB Soy Sauce	.15
1 pound assorted vegetables	2.00
¼ cup cheese, parmesan works best	.75
½ TB Worchester Sauce (optional)	.10
1/8 cup milk	.10
Total is $12.60 for 4 servings or $3.15 per serving	

Shepard's Pie Directions

Begin by "rough" peeling the potatoes. Russet potatoes have bitter skins, but the skins of red and golden potatoes are sweet, so you only need to peel ¾ off. The remaining peel will add color to your dish. Boil for 10 minutes or until soft. Add the butter or cream cheese and parmesan cheese. Beat. Then add the milk 1 TB at a time until you get the consistency you want. You don't want these runny as they have to stand up in your dish. Cook the hamburger. You will need hamburger and onion for the chili, so cook all the hamburger and onion that you need for both dishes together and then split. This will save you time. Whenever I cook hamburger, I always add another pound and put in a container so when I make spaghetti later on in the week, I only need to add the sauce. If you want to do that, cook 3 pounds and take one pound out for the spaghetti, before you add the onion. If you want to make this dish more vegetarian, substitute 1 cup cooked lentils and ½ pound hamburger/onion mixture for the pie. Put one half of the hamburger/onion mixture in a pot for the chili. To the hamburger for the pie, add 1 TB Soy Sauce, ½ TB Worchester sauce and ½ tsp salt. The Soy Sauce takes the place of a bouillon cube which is salt and msg. Take out an 8 x 8 inch pyrex dish and spread the hamburger on the bottom. I use frozen mixed vegetables for this dish as it saves me a lot of time. Vegetables should be diced small so that they will only take 15 minutes to cook. Then spread the mashed potatoes on top of the mixed vegetables and cover and put away in your fridge. When you are ready to eat, cook at 350 degrees for 10 minutes, then brown the top.

Chili

The chili is actually healthy because you are not using canned tomatoes which are very suspect in terms of what may have leaked into them. The reason why spaghetti sauce is in glass jars is because of how acid tomatoes are. They eat through the lining of cans and the chemicals in the lining go into your food, so it is a good idea to either make dishes that call for tomatoes from scratch or use brands like Bionaturae organic tomato paste in a glass jar. It is so concentrated that you will only use ½ of the $3.50, 7 oz jar. Because you are making chili from scratch, in order to have your fresh tomatoes taste "stewed," that all chili recipes call for, you will need to simmer in a crock pot or pan for at least half an hour. If you have children the effort will be well worth it as young children and teens love chili.

Chili Directions

Soak 3 cups of Kidney beans overnight, pour off the water and then put the beans in a crock pot and cook all day with four times the water to beans ratio. Or you can simmer in a pot for an hour. Simmer means you brought your food to a boil, then turned down the heat, so it is slightly boiling.

Drain the beans and add in the hamburger/onion mixture that you have left over from the Shepard's pie. Add in all the other ingredients and bring to a boil. Taste it. If too rich, add a little water. If not spicy enough, add some more chili powder, etc. Write down what you changed so you have created your own chili recipe that works for you. My teen loves chili so when I cook the beans, I make enough for three batches and freeze two batches. Then all I need to do next time I cook chili is pull out the beans, sauté the meat and onions and throw everything in the pot and bring to a boil. It takes me 15 minutes.

Chili	Organic Budget
1 pound of hamburger	$7.00
½ onion	1.00
2 tomatoes	1.00
3 cups cooked kidney beans	1.05
2 cloves garlic	.10
1/2 cup water if using tomato paste	
1/2 tsp salt	.15
¼ to ½ tsp cayenne (optional)	.10
½ quart of unseasoned tomato sauce in a jar	2.50
or	
3.5 oz tomato paste plus 2 tsp chili powder (taste and adjust)	
Plus ½ tsp sugar if tomato paste had no sweetener, not needed if you used tomato sauce.	
This makes 4 pounds of chili and is very filling at $ 12.90 which is $3.22 per serving.	

Latin Salad

Do you like bowls that you can buy at so many places now? Well you can make them using organic ingredients, for less money and with the ingredients you like. So what do you like?.....corn, black or pinto beans, red onions, avocado, tomatoes, cilantro? Put what you like in a bowl. What really gives this salad flavor is the blackened chicken or fish and the sauce. To make blackened chicken or fish, simply purchase "blackened" seasoning and coat the thinly sliced meat and lightly fry on both sides. Then cover and cook over medium heat for a few minutes until done. Add your meat and sauce to the salad bowl and you will have a great meal that you could easily get addicted to for @$4.00.

Salad Ingredients	Organic Budget
3 oz fish or chicken	$1.50
½ head lettuce	.85
¼ cup corn	.25
1 cup beans and rice	.25
Avocado, cheese, onion, cilantro, etc.	1.50

Sauce
1 TB mayonnaise
½ TB sour cream
¼ clove garlic
¼ tsp fresh lime juice
Dash of cayenne

CHAPTER TWELVE- MAIN MEALS FOUR

Chicken Alfredo, Cheesy Potato Casserole, Vegetable Wok

I often work long hours so when my children became 12 and I could trust them to heat up food, I would often make Chicken Cacciatore, Chicken Alfredo or Spaghetti and noodles before I would go to work. Once you know how to make a dish like that, it only takes 10 to 15 minutes to put it together and then while the dish would simmer for 10 to 15 minutes, I would put on my makeup and get dressed. Once it was done, I would put the sauce and noodles in the fridge in the same pan I had cooked the sauce in. All my children had to do was heat up the noodles and sauce and I had a great meal when I got home. All I had to do was add a vegetable to achieve my acid/alkaline balance.

The secret to always having great meals available is to think ahead two to three days so you know what to shop for or take out what you need, like some frozen chicken the night before. The same could be said for making a stew, curry, Quinoa muffins etc. Any one of them could be made in 10 to 15 minutes before you go to work and simmer or cook while you are getting dressed. The only challenge has been to train my children to use a low flame to heat up the sauce. Being kids, they want their food NOW and would cook everything on the highest flame possible and burn everything. Rice noodles tend to stick and you don't want to boil them in tap water or they will absorb all the impurities in the water. The most efficient way to cook them is to add 1TB of oil per pound of noodles to the cooking water and stir often.

Chicken Alfredo	Organic Budget
1 cup heavy cream or half and half	$1.15
½ pound chicken	3.50
1 clove garlic, crushed	.10
1/4 cup butter	.75
1.5 cups Parmesan cheese	1.50
12 ounces rice noodles	4.00
Total is $11 divided by 2 servings or $5.50 per serving	

Directions for Alfredo

This is not a budget meal but worth making once in a while if you like rich dishes. Melt the butter and sauté the chicken and garlic. Add 1/3 cup water and boil until the water is gone. Add the cream and Parmesan cheese. Salt and pepper to taste. Put your noodles on a plate and pour the sauce over it. Add a vegetable side dish to make more alkaline.

Cheesy Potato Casserole Directions

There are lots of recipes for this type of casserole on the web. Simply combine all the ingredients together and bake at 350 for 40 minutes. This could be a side dish to serve with a small portion of meat, like your grilled chicken. Then add a fairly large portion of vegetables to achieve your acid/alkaline balance. You will be using two cups of your favorite cheese, cut in small cubes. This could be a combination of several cheeses like Cheddar, Mozzarella, Swiss, Ricotta, etc. If you use Ricotta, don't use more than 1 cup. I prefer Pepper Jack cheese for this dish. You could try different combinations every time you make this for variety. The cheese already has a lot of salt in it, so you don't need much additional salt.

Cheesy Potato Casserole	Organic Budget
6 large red potatoes, peeled and cut into 3/4 inch cubes	$2.50
1 cup parmesan cheese	2.00
1 cup sour cream	1.50
4 green onions, finely chopped	.50
3 tablespoons chopped fresh parsley or cilantro	.10
1 tsp dried basil	.05
2 TB minced fresh garlic	.10
2 cups cheese	5.00
1/4 teaspoon paprika	.05
Total is $11.80 divided by 4 servings is @$3 per serving which is @1.5 pounds of food	

Tofu Vegetable, Chicken Wok Directions

There are a few good reasons to incorporate organic tofu into your diet. For one, tofu is alkaline while meat is acid. Tofu has about half the protein of meat and cost about half as much, ounce for ounce. However if what you want is bulk, meaning foods to fill you up for less money, then tofu is the better choice. Take the organic tofu and cut in half lengthwise so it is one inch thick. Fry lightly on each side. Take out of the pan and set on a paper towel on a plate. Put the vegetables you want to use in your food processor and chop. Sauté the vegetables with the garlic and chicken. Add the chicken broth and steam until almost done. Add the tofu, soy sauce, sugar and scallions and turn off the flame. Best if you don't cook the scallions all the way. Serve over rice or noodles.

Tofu Vegetable, Chicken Wok	Organic Budget
1-10 oz package of tofu	$2.00
2 pounds of vegetables, broccoli, cauliflower, etc.	4.00
4 ounces of chicken	1.75
1 TB Soy sauce	.15
1 tsp sugar	.10
3 scallions	.25
2 TB oil to cook.	.25
6 cups of rice	1.50
Total $10 divided by 4 servings is $2.50 per serving.	

CHAPTER THIRTEEN- MAIN MEALS FIVE

Spinach Lasagna, Pizza and Squash Soups

For this session you will be making spaghetti sauce for both the Lasagna and the Pizza, so make enough for a third meal and freeze it for the future. The lasagna is not a $4 meal, so if you need to stay under the $10 a day budget, then eat less expensive meals for the rest of the day. Lasagna and pizza are a tad time consuming, but the soups are quick. Both the lasagna and pizza are acidic meals so balance with vegetables or a salad. You can find recipes for vegetable side dishes in Chapter Eighteen. Yes, you are adding spinach to the lasagna and vegetables to the pizza, but if you remember from the first chapter, alkaline foods such as vegetables need to be 45% of the meal. So pull out your music or TV show or whatever you use to entertain yourself while you cook and have fun.

You will be making a new soup as a meal. Soups are easy to make acid/alkaline balanced because they are made up mostly of beans and vegetables. Squash soups are so delicious and by adding some beans to your soup and a side of bread like cornbread or muffins, you have a meal. The first soup, which is a cream soup is not a meal, but serves as a vegetable side dish to any meal. Once you have added a little sugar, nutmeg and cream or milk, you have a soup that will satisfy your sweet tooth and still score fairly low on the glycemic index. Since the soup is in the middle of the acid/alkaline scale, it also makes a great snack. If you don't like having to cut off the skin from the squash which is a little tedious, you can bake the night before and then easily scoop the squash out of the shell. If your squash and beans are pre-cooked, you could easily make the soups on the next page in less than 15 minutes. For variety you can try cooking more than one soup. Once you have your cutting board out and have set out all your ingredients, it only takes a few more minutes to make the second or third soup. You will need garbanzo beans (chick peas) for both this chapter and for the Quinoa salad in the next chapter, so make up enough beans for these two dishes and a couple containers to freeze for future salads and soups.

Lasagna Ingredients	Organic Budget
1 pound of hamburger (add in another half pound for the pizza)	$7.00
1 quart of pasta sauce (add in another half quart for the pizza)	4.50
½ pound of lasagna noodles	1.00
1 pound of ricotta cheese	6.00
½ pound of cheddar cheese	3.50
½ cup parmesan cheese	1.00
Vegetables like spinach, pepper, mushrooms, etc. (optional)	
Total is $23 divided by @5 pounds or 5 servings is $4.60.	

Lasagna Directions

Start by boiling water for the noodles. Set aside 1/2 cup tomato sauce and 3 TB parmesan cheese. Add the noodles to the water and cook until slightly under done. Sauté the hamburger until done and add the remaining spaghetti sauce and parmesan cheese. Take out 1/3 for the pizza and set aside in a bowl. If you are adding vegetables like spinach, green pepper and/or mushrooms to the lasagna, then add them to the spaghetti sauce and cook for two minutes. Add the grated cheddar cheese to the ricotta cheese, mix and set aside. In your cooking dish, add a little of the spaghetti sauce that you set aside to the bottom of your dish. If you put the noodles down first, then they will burn. Layer the noodles on top of the sauce. Then layer the cheese. Add another layer of noodles and then the remaining spaghetti sauce. Add the final layer of noodles and spread the ¼ cup of tomato sauce that you set aside on top and sprinkle the 3 TB parmesan cheese. Cover and put in the fridge. You only need to cook for 15 minutes at 350 to heat up the lasagna when you are ready to eat.

Directions for the Pizza

This is in not a dish that you want to make for the first time for a dinner party. Not everyone likes gluten free pizza crust because you can't get the hard chewy texture that most people expect without using gluten. You have to use white rice flour or your dough will be too gritty. You can purchase organic, gluten free pizza mixes online if you find making pizza dough tricky. You need to choose if you want to use yeast or buttermilk to make your dough rise. Put the warm water, sugar and yeast in a cup or use buttermilk by putting 1 tsp vinegar in 1/3 cup milk.

Mix together the dry ingredients. Then mix in the oil, yeast water or buttermilk. All dry ingredients should be wet so if necessary, add water 1 TB at a time. Let rise for an hour. Put your dough between two pieces of parchment paper and roll out to 1/8 inch thick. Gluten free dough is slightly wetter than what you may be use to so don't be tempted to add flour to make it too dry.

Line a pan with parchment paper and cook the pizza crust at 450 degrees for 5 minutes without the sauce. You can transfer to a pizza stone at this point if you like, but not necessary. Take out of the oven and spread the spaghetti sauce over your pizza shell. Add vegetables like mushrooms, pepper, thinly sliced zucchini, etc. Top with the grated cheddar cheese and cook at 350 for another 10 minutes. Crust should be brown on the bottom. Watch it, as it burns easily.

Pizza Dough Ingredients	Organic Budget
1 cup baking mix	$1.25
1 cup white rice flour	1.00
1/2 tsp sugar	.05
3 TB olive oil	.30
1/3 cup buttermilk	.20
or 1 tsp yeast plus 1 tsp sugar in 1/3 cup water	
Total is $2.80 for the crust	
Sauce	
Spaghetti sauce with meat or chicken	$5.00
Assorted vegetables for toppings like mushrooms, green and red pepper, broccoli, pineapple, fresh tomatoes, etc.	1.00
½ pound cheese	3.50
Total $9.50 for the topping plus the crust is $12.30 for 4 servings is $3.10, 2 slices per serving.	

Cream of Squash Soup 1

2 TB butter

½ onion

1 large butternut squash

½ tsp salt

¼ tsp pumpkin pie spice

¼ tsp cinnamon

½ cup cream or half and half

Chopped apple

½ cup chicken broth

1 TB Sugar

Chicken Garbanzo Soup 2

1 TB olive oil

1 small red onion

1.25 cups cooked chick peas

¾ pounds chicken

½ cup corn

1 TB curry powder

½ tsp salt

½ cup butternut squash

1 carton chicken broth

1 TB sugar

Shrimp Squash Soup 3

1 TB olive oil

1 medium onion

1 clove minced garlic

1 cup cubed, peeled butternut squash

½ green pepper

4 ounces shelled shrimp

1.5 cups cooked chickpeas

½ cup corn

1 medium tomato

2 tsp basil

1/2 tsp oregano

1/4 tsp cayenne pepper

1 bay leaf

1/4 cup parmesan cheese

1 carton low sodium broth

½ tsp sugar

Directions for the Soups

In this section you have three quick soups you can make. Soups 2 and 3 are a meal in themselves. I love this recipe for Cream of Squash Soup, but cutting the squash up can be a chore, so I developed a quick way to do it. Just cook the squash in the oven, seeds and all for 20 minutes at 350, then cut it. For soup 1, sauté the onion in the butter, add in the rest of the ingredients and boil for a few minutes. Transfer to a blender and blend until smooth. If needed, thin with soup stock or half and half. If you like nutmeg, then add a dash to each soup.

For soup 2, sauté the chicken and onion. Add in the rest of the ingredients and boil for 3 minutes. If peeling the squash is a chore, then use the method for soup 1 for soups 2 and 3. Just cook for 15 minutes instead of 30.

For soup 3, sauté the onion, garlic, pepper and squash in the olive oil for 5 minutes. Add the shrimp and sauté for 1 minute. Add the rest of the ingredients except for the parmesan cheese and boil for another three minutes. When you serve the soup, sprinkle the parmesan cheese on top.

CHAPTER FOURTEEN- MAIN MEALS SIX

Chicken Cacciatore, Thai Curry, Quinoa Salad

This session is designed to teach you how to cook several meals when you have less than an hour to cook. You will begin by sautéing an onion and chicken and then adding your choice of vegetables and steam with some chicken broth. Then you will divide the chicken/vegetable mixture into three bowls to make three different sauces. The whole process will take you less than an hour. These sauces get better over time and will keep for up to five days. I personally don't think freezing vegetables after you cook them tastes good, but you may feel differently. If that works for you, then you can make several servings and freeze them. You can create more variety by serving over different grains or different types of noodles.

I like to use raw food garnishes when I serve my food, to get the enzymes and vitamin C that cooking often destroys. So try cutting up some red pepper and add it raw to the chicken cacciatore and some parsley when you are ready to serve. If you haven't already cooked the garbanzo beans and quinoa, then soak and cook so you can make the salad at another time.

Asian and Indian cuisines are all far less acidic than the standard American diet. If you use brown rice instead of white, you will make your meals more alkaline and nutritious. In this chapter, I will introduce you to a Thai staple that you can incorporate into your diet for variety and maybe inspire you to go online and try more Asian recipes as it is easier to achieve a healthy acid/alkaline balance with Indian and Asian foods than many "American" type dishes. If you have never had Thai curry and there is a Thai restaurant in your city, then go try a meal and see if you like it. If you do, then you can make the dish at home. What I love about the internet is that you can find any recipe you want and I like the challenge of trying to make something at home that I loved in a restaurant. "Thai and True Curries" are organic and can be ordered through Amazon. In addition to introducing you to Thai food, in this chapter you will be making another great salad that is a meal. So let's start cooking!

Chicken Cacciatore	Organic Budget
1 pound chicken cut in small chunks	$7.00
½ onion	.50
2 garlic cloves	.10
4 cups vegetables, Cauliflower, zucchini, bell pepper, broccoli work well	4.00
2 TB tomato paste	.50
2 cups chicken broth	1.00
2 potatoes	1.00
3 TB oil	1.00
1 TB Italian Seasoning	.10
½ tsp salt	.05
12 ounces rice noodles	4.00
Total is $19.25 for 4 servings is $4.81. Price drops to $4 if you serve with rice instead of noodles.	

Directions for the Chicken Cacciatore

If you are making all three dishes, then sauté 1.5 pounds chicken with 1 onion. Then transfer 1/3 of the chicken/onion mixture into another pan for the Thai curry. In the Cacciatore pan add the thick vegetables that take longer to cook like cauliflower, carrots and broccoli and sauté for 3 minutes and add 1/3 cup water and steam. Then add the rest of the vegetables and sauté for a minute. Add the broth, spices and tomato paste. Bring to a boil and simmer for 10 minutes or until vegetables are almost done. Serve one cup of cacciatore over two cups of rice of noodles to achieve your acid/alkaline balance. I prefer quinoa/rice noodles.

Directions for the Curry Sauce

Add the vegetables from page 74 to the onion/chicken mixture and sauté, then steam until done. Pour a small amount into two separate bowls. In one bowl add a tiny bit of peanut butter. Taste it. Do you like Thai peanut curry sauce? In the second bowl, add 1/4 tsp fish sauce and pinch basil. This is Thai Red Curry sauce. Now you get to decide. Do you only like the Red Thai curry? If so, only make that. If you like both curries, then split the chicken vegetable mixture into two containers and in one add 1 TB peanut butter. Taste and adjust the peanut butter until it tastes good. In the second bowl, add 1 TB fish sauce and some basil. When you are ready to eat, you will need to simmer for a couple minutes until sauce gets thick. Personally I prefer using two cups coconut milk instead of the chicken broth for the curries. The sauce is richer and more nutritious.

Red Thai Curry and Peanut Curry	Organic Budget
½ pound chicken	$3.50
2.5 cups vegetables, Bok Choy, cauliflower, summer squash etc. work well	2.00
1 TB Thai curry sauce	.65
1 TB brown sugar	.10
1.5 cups coconut milk	2.00
½ cup chicken broth	1.00
1/8 tsp stevia	.10
1/3 tsp salt	.10
1 TB Peanut Butter (optional) or	.10
1 TB fish sauce (optional)	.10
Total is $9.65 for 3 servings is $3.22 plus 2 cups rice per serving is $3.92 total.	

Quinoa or Millet Garbanzo Bean Greek Salad

This salad has become popular in many restaurants because it is really delicious and it will fill you up. Most restaurants charge $10 to $12 for this salad. Your cost will be less than $4 if you use millet and less than $5 if you use quinoa. Organic quinoa costs almost $8 a pound, while millet cost $2 a pound uncooked. The difference in cost is pretty insignificant as you will need less than a quarter of a pound for each salad. Both quinoa and millet are very light grains which make them ideal for a salad. So pick a theme. I like Greek, so I add garbanzo beans, tomato, feta cheese, Greek olives, red onion, green pepper and sun dried tomatoes to my greens.

Try using a poultry scissors to cut up dried, sun dried tomatoes rather than cutting with a knife. I season with Olive oil and lemon juice. You can use rice instead of millet or quinoa if you like. The possibilities are endless. To make this a meal, you need to use 1/2 head of lettuce, 1 cup of grain and 1/3 cup of beans plus 1/3 pound cheese/meat plus your condiments. This salad is a meal and if you like, you can serve with cornbread or muffins and use less grain in your salad.

CHAPTER FIFTEEN – MAIN MEALS SEVEN

Sushi, Chicken Pot Pie, Macaroni and Cheese

There are several you-tube videos on how to make sushi that would be helpful to watch if you are making this for the first time. We are including this simple dish in this book because many people love sushi and it takes two minutes to make once you have your rice cooked and your vegetables cut up. We will start with a variation of the classic California roll. From there you can look up recipes online and experiment with peanut butter and jelly sushi, walnut and edame (raw soy beans) sushi, etc. You need to presoak your rice as outlined in Chapter Eight as brown rice that has not been soaked is too hard for sushi. You will also need a sushi mat, Nori sheets, the hot green paste and fresh ginger, so look for it in the Asian section of your local supermarket or order online so you have this ready. The first time you make this you need to allow time to figure it out. Once you do, the effort will be well worth it as sushi is really delicious and the Nori seaweed provides a lot of important minerals that you need in your diet.

Sushi Directions

Cook your soaked brown rice with the white rice and let sit until cool enough to handle. In a small saucepan, combine the rice vinegar, oil, sugar and ¼ tsp salt over medium heat until the sugar dissolves. Pour ¾ over the rice and keep stirring until the rice dries. Consistency should be sticky and moist but not soggy. If not wet enough, add the rest of the sugar, vinegar mix 1 TB at a time until you achieve the consistency you are looking for. Place the Nori sheet on top of your Shushi mat. Spread the rice ¼ inch thick on top of the Nori using a wooden

Sushi Rice

1 cup brown rice

2 cups white rice

3.5 cups water

1/3 cup rice vinegar

1 TB vegetable oil

1/4 cup white sugar

paddle. If using shrimp, crabmeat or salmon, mix first with a little mayonnaise. Add cucumber, avocado, sesame seeds, diced scallions if you like on top of the rice and roll. If you want the rice on the outside, then flip the Nori with the rice on top, over, then add your condiments and roll. The more vegetables you add, the more alkaline the dish. So experiment with adding green pepper, zucchini, carrots, steamed asparagus, etc. You can make or purchase pickled ginger and hot paste to serve this with. The hot paste you can order as a powder online. The pickled ginger you can make if you can't find it locally. If not, then you can find a recipe online and make it up a couple of days in advance.

The imitation crab meat has ingredients in there that I can't spell so I would recommend not using it. If you can't afford real crab, then try shrimp. Don't cook your rice until you are ready to eat. If the rice gets hard in the fridge, it won't work and if you try resteaming it, it will be too wet. You have to use white rice or the sushi will be too grainy. Before you roll the sushi, taste the rice. It doesn't have to taste plain. Get creative and season it. I add diced sun dried tomatoes, red pepper, Greek olives and red onions to the rice with Italian seasoning and a ½ cup mayonnaise. It is awesome!

Sushi Filling Ingredients	Sushi Dipping Sauce	Budget for Two Rolls	
½ cucumber, peeled, cut into small strips	1 cup water	Filling	$1 to $2.00
½ avocado	1/4 cup Mirin, Japanese wine	Sushi Rice	.75
½ pound shrimp	2 tablespoons soy sauce	2 sheets Nori	.70
Mayonnaise	1/2 tsp rice wine vinegar	Dipping Sauce	.70
Scallions, etc.	Wisk together and enjoy!	Ginger, hot paste, etc.	.40
		Total @$4 or $2 per roll	

Chicken Pot Pie Directions

For this dish, since you will be cooking diced chicken and onions, you could easily cook an additional 1 cup and make a Cream of Broccoli casserole. If you already have cream of chicken soup in your freezer, all you would need is some cooked rice, parmesan cheese and a stalk of broccoli. It will only add another 5 to 10 minutes to add the Cream of Broccoli casserole. For the pot pie, mix 1 TB cornstarch to 3TB soup stock and set aside. Once you have completed sautéing the chicken and onion, add the frozen peas, millet, carrots corn starch and the soup stock. Bring almost to a boil then add to your oven containers. You can put on the lid and freeze any you won't be eating right away. When you are ready to eat, make up some pie crust. The recipe is at the end of Chapter Nineteen. You can either pat down the dough on top

or roll out to 1/8 inch thick and place on top of the filling. Crust tends to burn on the rim, so I scrape it off. This whole process works best if you make the crust when you are ready to eat. Cook at 350 degrees for 20 minutes. While the chicken pot pie ingredients do well in the fridge, the crust does not. It gets soggy if it sits on top of the wet ingredients.

Chicken Pot Pie Ingredients	Organic Budget
1 pound chicken	$7.00
1 small onion	.75
1 pd bag of peas and carrots	2.25
half a carton of chicken broth	2.00
1 TB cornstarch	.05

Total is $12.30 divided by 4 is $3.07 plus 50 cents per pie for crust.

Crust- See "Let's Bake" Chapter for Pie Crust recipe. Make half the recipe.

Macaroni and Cheese Directions

Sometimes you just want comfort food, well you can have it. My mom use to make macaroni and cheese for us all the time, so I crave it. In this recipe you will make it gluten free with organic ingredients. You just need to balance the acidity of this dish with a vegetable/fruit smoothie sometime during the day. Boil your gluten free noodles until they are done, but not soft. While you are waiting for your noodles to boil, start making the sauce. Melt the butter over a very low heat. Add the milk and cheese. Stir often. Keep the heat low. You don't want to boil the cheese or it separates. Once the cheese has melted, then take the flour and add 3 TB of milk and make a paste. Add to the sauce mix and stir. Salt and pepper to taste. Then pour over the noodles. You can serve like this or cook in the oven in a pyrex dish for 10 minutes so it thickens a bit.

Macaroni and Cheese Ingredients	Budget
12 oz of rice noodles	$4.00
½ cube of butter	.75
1 cup half and half	1.00
2 TB rice or potato flour	.05
½ pound cheese cut in chunks	3.50

Total is $9.30 divided by 2 servings is $4.65 per servings. Divide by 3 and add vegetables for a healthier and more economical meal.

CHAPTER SIXTEEN

Breakfast

All these breakfasts take 5 minutes if you have already put together your protein drink powder, the organic gluten free pancake and waffle mix and pre-cooked your whole oats. Depending on what you put in your protein drink, that will determine your price. Mine cost me @$2 for a large scoop. The hearty oatmeal will cost you $1.50 if you use organic milk or 50 cents less if you use water. A large waffle will cost you $2.00 including the cost of the syrup if you make your own. Waffle batter should be almost runny. If too thin add 1 TB of brown rice flour, 1 TB at a time. If too thick add in more milk, 1 TB at a time. If your waffle is too dense, then next time add ¼ tsp baking powder or another egg. If you want your waffles to be heavier, then add an additional ½ cup sorghum or rice flour to the baking mix.

These are better if you use buttermilk because the lactic acid in buttermilk is a leavening (rising) agent. To make buttermilk, simply add 1 TB lemon juice or vinegar to 1 cup milk and wait 5 minutes. If you make waffles and pancakes a lot, then buy organic butter milk. If you seldom make them or can't find organic butter milk, then use this tip. If you can taste the vinegar, then use a little less next time.

If you tried to buy organic pure maple syrup, you probably hesitated when you saw the cost. The reason why we are adding Stevia and sugar to the waffle mix is so that you only need 1 -2 TB's of syrup per large waffle or 4 pancake stack, instead of three times that much. It will be just as satisfying as using a lot of syrup. You want to avoid commercial brands of syrup as they often

Pancake and Waffle Mix

5 cups baking mix from Chapter 19

1 cup sorghum flour

1/2 tsp Stevia

1/4 cup Sugar

Store in an air tight container.

When you are ready to make pancakes or waffles, just combine the wet ingredients on the next page with 1 cup of your pancake and waffle mix.

Pancake and Waffles

1 cup waffle mix

1 egg

1.25 cups buttermilk (coconut milk)

1 TB Oil

Syrup

1 cup water

3/4 cup organic, fair trade white sugar

3/4 cup organic brown sugar

1 tablespoon maple flavored extract

½ tsp Stevia

use corn syrup. Non-organic corn products are GMO products. If you are on a strict budget, then make your own maple syrup. Bring all the ingredients except the maple flavoring from the list to the left, to a boil. Turn the heat down to low and simmer 1 minute. Add in the maple flavoring, turn off the heat and let cool.

My favorite way of eating waffles is pictured above. I use 1 tsp sugar with 1 TB sour cream and fresh strawberries. 1 tsp of sugar is 16 grams of carbohydrates.

If you look at your syrup bottles, one serving is 53 grams of carbohydrates which is why people crash in the afternoon or drink tons of coffee. Both the sugar and the caffeine will exhaust your adrenals and pancreas making one a prime candidate for diabetes and low blood sugar.

What about the fat in the sour cream? If you notice throughout this book there is very little dairy used, so enjoy.

Hearty Oatmeal

1 cup pre-cooked oat groats or steel cut oats

1/3 cup oatmeal

1 cup milk or water

1TB brown sugar

½ tsp Fair Trade cinnamon

Pinch salt and stevia

Oatmeal Directions

If you like this oatmeal, then cook up the oat groats or steel cut oats in advance. By taking care of this step in advance, it will only take you 5 minutes to make this oatmeal. Rinse the oat groats, then add water so water is 1 inch above the top of the whole oats in your rice cooker. Store in a container when done. To make the oatmeal, put all ingredients from the menu to the left in a pot and bring to a boil. Turn off the heat or transfer to another burner if you are using an electric stove. Go take a shower or answer your emails for five minutes while the oatmeal thickens. Then serve.

Protein Drink

Every day should start with a high protein breakfast because it boosts your metabolism which helps you feel energetic and alert. The best way to accomplish this without the bulk of a heavy breakfast, which will make you feel sluggish, is with a protein drink. You can purchase high quality organic protein powder at a reasonable price at www.truenutrition.com. You can use this code "jdk" for a 10% discount. The reason why the prices are reasonable for organic or non-GMO protein is because you aren't paying for packaging and advertising.

Make sure you include the "Super Greens" powder, @10% so that you get your greens every day and it makes the drink more alkaline. The Grass Fed whey insures you get vitamin K2. Add a little flax seeds for fiber and Chia Seeds for energy and fiber. I am suggesting a little, because un-soaked seeds have phytic acid in them. You need fiber to keep you "regular" every day so that you are eliminating toxins, otherwise you may be sluggish, tired and sick often. By including fiber in your drink you won't have to think about it. Put your own personal mix together in an air tight container. When you are ready to use, add 1/8 teaspoon stevia, a little fresh fruit and half a banana and you will be in heaven while consuming over 20 grams of protein for @$2.50 a drink and it is really filling. This drink is higher in nutrients than a waffle or oatmeal. If you are trying to lose weight, make your drink with water. If you are trying to gain weight, use milk and a banana.

Egg Biscuits

Whisk together equal parts eggs, rice flour and milk. In other words, if you have half a cup of eggs, then add ½ cup milk and ½ cup rice flour. Add ¼ tsp salt and 1 tsp melted butter for every two eggs you use. Pour half full, into a greased muffin tin and bake at 400 degrees for 20 to 30 minutes. Let cool for 5 minutes before trying to get out of the pan. They will rise and then fall after they cool. This is suppose to happen. These egg biscuits are like little quiches. You can add a little chopped onion, green pepper and cayenne if you like.

Breakfast Muffins

Use the recipe from Chapter Nineteen for gluten free quinoa or millet bread and add raisins, nuts, dried fruit, etc. to make breakfast muffins. The whole grain in these muffins will provide a texture similar to a bran muffin without the wheat.

CHAPTER SEVENTEEN

Sauces and Soups

Sauces

If you like meals with noodles, it is best to use organic rice noodles. Best price is on brands distributed by the store itself like Trader Joes. The Pasta meals are $4 for 1 pound of food cooked if you use rice noodles as they are more expensive than wheat noodles. Balance out the meat and cheese sauce meals with a salad or a vegetable as both those sauces are very acidic. Noodles are slightly acid. Cook in this order in order to get your meal to the table in 20 minutes. First start the water boiling for the pasta. Use a lid so it heats faster and add noodles when water comes to a boil. Then start the sauce. In between stirring the sauce, you can make the salad. Make triple what you need for the sauces and store in the freezer. I save jelly jars to use for sauce storage. Best to freeze any sauce that you won't be using up in 5 days. The barbecue sauce will last at least two weeks and given how often corn syrup is used in barbecue sauce, it is a good idea to have this on hand.

5 Minute Barbecue Sauce	Organic Budget
1-10 oz container of organic catsup	$3.50
2 TB organic molasses	.50
1 TB vinegar	
2 TB of a seasoning mix. like Mesquite chicken/steak seasoning, etc.	

Directions for the Barbecue Sauce

Bring all ingredients to a boil and turn off the heat. Taste it. If you want it richer, then add more molasses, 1 tsp at a time. If you want it spicier, add a little cayenne pepper. If you want it a little sharper, add ½ tsp vinegar. If sauce is too bland, then add more of your seasoning mix. Read the ingredients in the seasoning mix and make sure it doesn't contain msg. Write down what you did, so next time you make it, you won't need to spend the time to figure out how to get it right for what works for you. If you are on a budget and you rarely barbecue, then don't worry about the molasses being organic. If you barbecue all the time, then purchasing organic molasses is a good investment in your health as molasses is rich in iron. Organic catsup goes on sale all the time so when it does, buy a bunch!

Meat Marinades

Most likely you have your favorite meat marinades. However with organic cooking, given how expensive ingredients like oil is, you won't be covering your meat with the marinade. You will make it and dip your meat in it, then pile your sections of meat on top of each other and let sit for half an hour. I use this recipe for three pounds of chicken. Combine the ingredients with seasonings that you like. Try 1 Tb Italian seasoning. If you want a spicier meat, then add ½ tsp cumin, 1 tsp chili powder, 1 tsp oregano and a small dried chili. You can also add your favorite rub or seasoning mix like Mesquite seasoning, just make sure it doesn't contain msg. Marinade costs @$1.50

Marinade Ingredients

¼ cup oil

1 tsp salt

1 TB vinegar

garlic

onion (optional)

3 Minute Sun Dried Tomato Mayonnaise

1/2 cup mayonnaise

2 teaspoons sun-dried tomatoes, minced

1 teaspoon Italian seasoning

½ teaspoon fresh lemon juice

½ clove garlic

6 Minute Alfredo Sauce

1/4 cup butter

1 cup heavy cream or half and half

1 clove garlic, crushed

1 1/2 cups freshly grated Parmesan cheese

Dash of pepper

Directions for the Mayonnaise

Combine all ingredients and put in a jar. Best if you let it sit for a day in the fridge. If you like hot and spicy, then add a little salsa and red pepper to the mayonnaise instead of the lemon juice. Don't make it too watery as you can use this for flat bread vegetable sandwiches and you don't want to soak the bread. It is also good as a marinade for vegetable and shrimp sushi.

Directions for Alfredo Sauce

While the butter is melting over low heat, chop up the garlic and add to the butter. Add cream and parmesan cheese. Whisk often as you bring almost to a boil. Let cool and put in a glass jar. This sauce freezes well. When you are ready to make Chicken Alfredo, all you have to do is add cooked chicken and pour over noodles. If you like parsley, then add a pinch.

2 Minute Yogurt Curry Sauce
1 cup Yogurt
1 tsp curry powder
¼ tsp salt

3 Minute Teriyaki Sauce
1/2 cup soy sauce
1/4 cup water
2 tablespoons sweet rice wine
¼ cup brown sugar
¼ tsp Stevia

Directions for Curry Sauce

Mix together all ingredients and use in soups that can then be used as a sauce over rice or as a dip or a spread for sandwiches or even in vegetable sushi. Add a little sugar if you like.

Directions for Teriyaki Sauce

This sauce is great over chicken in your bowls. Simply bring the ingredients to a boil, turn off the heat and store in a jar once it cools. You are welcome to add ginger, garlic, cayenne, etc.

Soups

Beans are mildly acidic. Similar to what you did for the lentil soup in Chapter Ten, all you need to do is add vegetables and you will have a perfectly balanced soup that can be eaten as a meal or snack. There are online recipes using black beans with some stew meat and Mexican seasonings. Garnish with avocado, cilantro and lime juice. Try garbanzo beans mixed with corn and other sweet vegetables, etc. Make three times as many beans as you need as beans freeze well and you can use them in bowls, soups, dips, etc. Soak beans overnight to get rid of the phytic acid. Drain the water off and put in a crock pot and cook all day or overnight. Drain and put in several containers. Beans will last a long time but the vegetables will not. When you are ready to eat the soup, in a sauce pan sauté half an onion, vegetables and meat. Add your chicken or beef broth and cook until done. Use 1 cup vegetables for ½ cup of beans. I prefer cauliflower, a little celery and carrots.

Directions to Make the Miso Soup

Break up the wakame in your hands into small pieces. In a bowl of water soak the wakame and shitake mushrooms for 10 minutes. In a pan sauté the onion and hard vegetables like carrots and cauliflower. Cut the tofu into squares and cut up the mushrooms into 4 pieces. Then add the mushrooms, wakame, tofu and soaking water to the pan and add enough water to cover and simmer for six minutes. Add in any green leafy vegetables like bokchoy and simmer for another 2 minutes. You don't want to completely cook your vegetables as you will be heating your soup up later which will cook the vegetables some more. When you are ready to serve, bring the portion you will be eating almost to a boil, then transfer to another burner. In a separate bowl, take 1 Tb of Miso and make into a paste with 2 TB of water. Ladle 1 cup vegetables with 1cup soup stock into the bowl with the miso. You aren't cooking the miso because you don't want to kill the enzymes.

Miso Soup	Organic Budget
1/2 package (10 oz) organic tofu	$1.00
1 piece wakame	.50
2 dried shitake mushrooms	.50
½ onion	.50
1 pound of assorted vegetables	2.00
1 TB Oil to sauté the vegetables in	.15
3 TB Organic Miso	1.00
Dash of Cayenne pepper (optional)	
Diced scallions for garnish	
4 servings divided by $5.65 is $1.41 per serving	

This miso soup is thick with vegetables and tofu. It is a meal by itself or snack. It is not like what you get in restaurants with only a few vegetables floating in it. Serve with brown rice and sunflower seeds for a completely balanced meal with 20 grams of protein based on ½ cup of tofu, 1 TB of sunflower seeds and 1.5 cups of brown rice. Total cost of the meal is around $2. It helps to get your children to eat it if you make a picture with your food, like I did here. Fruits and vegetables lend themselves to making all kinds of great pictures.

CHAPTER EIGHTEEN

Snacks and Side Dishes

Any side dish can be a snack. Most snacks can serve as a side dish. Many snacks can also be a light meal. You can look up "healthy snacks" on the web and come up with lots of ideas like yogurt with fruit with a little stevia in it. In keeping with our theme of quick and maintaining the acid/alkaline balance, following are some great snacks.

Chick Pea (Humus) Dip	Organic Budget
2 TB Tahini	$ .50
Juice from 1/3 to ½ lemon	.50
½ tsp salt	.10
1 cup garbanzo beans (chickpeas)	.35
Total is $1.45 for a little more than a cup of dip	

Humus with Chips Directions

Blend in a blender, ½ cup water with the tahini, lemon juice and salt. Add the beans. If you are using canned beans they often have salt in them, so blend first, then taste. Do you need more salt, lemon juice, some pepper? Then add. If too thick, then add more water 2 TB at a time. If too thin, then add more beans. Serve with chips or vegetables. Store the leftover dip in an air tight container. This will keep for at least five days, but does not freeze well. To achieve the acid/alkaline balance, all you need to do is eat equal portions of vegetables, fruit and chips.

Yogurt Dips

The Oikos Greek Yogurt Site has great ideas for using yogurt as a dip. In many recipes that call for mayonnaise, you can substitute yogurt. If you made your own yogurt as suggested in Chapter Six, it will cost you very little to make these healthy dips.

Fried Tofu with Ginger, Soy Sauce on Crackers

You can make some great snacks with crackers that can also double as a light meal. If you can't find gluten free crackers or they are too expensive, then you can make a flatbread using the pizza crust recipe in Chapter Thirteen. Add salt, sesame seeds and/or sunflower seeds and bake at 450 for 10 minutes. Tuna and cheese on crackers is great. To add more flavor to that snack, try adding sun dried tomatoes, capers, garlic, etc. You can always google "cracker snacks" to get more ideas. Just make sure you maintain the acid/alkaline balance by adding a vegetable dish.

First you need to decide how much tofu you will be eating. I eat one fourth of a 10 ounce package. To make the tofu with ginger as a cracker topping, cut the organic tofu in half lengthwise so it is one inch thick and fry it in a little oil until light brown. Drain on paper towels on a separate plate when done. While the tofu is cooking, make your sauce. Dice ½ scallion and add ¼ cup organic, wheat free soy sauce, 1 tsp sugar and ¼ inch fresh ginger and 1 clove garlic. Cut the tofu in squares and add the ginger, soy sauce and coat. Use as a topping for crackers. You can also add thinly sliced vegetables.

The cost is pretty much the cost of the tofu which is $1.99 to $2.50 for 10 ounces of organic tofu. You can make a lot of the ginger/soy sauce and store it, even freeze it. Then all you have to do when you want this again, is pull out the sauce and fry the tofu. You can expand this sauce by adding diced vegetables like peppers or even try a little avocado and see how you like it.

Fruit with Rice Pudding

I love fruit with Rice Pudding. If you make up the rice pudding in advance, then all you need to do when you are ready to eat is cut your fruit in half and add a scoop of rice pudding. While a little high on the glycemic index, this snack/desert provides body building protein and is balanced in terms of acid/alkaline if you only use ½ cup of rice pudding. It is also very filling. However given that this snack is high on the glycemic scale, eat midday not late in the evening. Pear, papaya, cantaloupe and mango all work well. If you don't want to make the rice pudding, then try ricotta cheese in the middle with a sprinkle of nutmeg.

The following rice pudding recipe is double what you will need for the fruit and rice pudding snack as I am assuming you will want to eat the pudding more than once. If not, then cut the recipe in half as this pudding does not freeze well. With all recipes I am going to assume that you have rice already made, so there won't be directions to make rice. Combine the cooked rice, milk, sugar, stevia and salt from the menu on the next page. Use your double boiler to keep from burning the pudding on the bottom. I love using a double boiler for puddings and sauces because they cook evenly. Once the water in the bottom has started to boil, turn down the heat to medium and cook until thick, about 15 to 20 minutes. Stir in the beaten egg and raisins. Cook 2 minutes more, stirring constantly. Remove from heat and stir in the butter and vanilla. When you are ready to serve, add to a scooped out fruit and sprinkle some cinnamon and/or nutmeg on top. In order to use the pudding for the fruit, you need to let it cool in the fridge so it has a little more body. After it gets cold, you should have no problem getting it to stand up in the fruit. If too watery, then add a little cooked rice.

Rice Pudding	Organic Budget
2 cups milk	$ 1.20
1.5 cups cooked long grain brown rice	.35
4 TB sugar	.50
¼ tsp Stevia	.15
¼ tsp salt	.05
1 egg	.40
1/2 cup raisins	.50
1 TB butter	.20
1/2 tsp vanilla	.05
Total is $3.40 divided by 4 servings is 85 cents per serving	

Vegetable Side Dishes

Sweet Potatoes

This root vegetable is full of nutrition and close to the middle for both acid/alkaline but a little high on the glycemic index.   For that reason they make a good snack but not a meal. Yams are becoming popular in health food restaurants as sweet potato fries. The problem with baked yams is that they take a long time to cook, so best to pre-cook them until almost done in an oven at 350 degrees for 45 minutes. Then you only need to heat up for 5 minutes for a snack. Serve with butter, salt, sour cream or if you want to avoid dairy, then fry them in a little oil with salt.

Asparagus with Lemon Juice and Salt

Sauté asparagus in a pan with 1 tsp of oil.   Once it is lightly brown, add ¼ cup water and steam until done. You can season with salsa or sun dried tomato mayonnaise or try lemon and salt or you can look up Hollandaise sauce online and make some for this dish.

Steamed Vegetables

If you steam vegetables, then drown them in butter and salt it kind of defeats the purpose of having a vegetable.   A better way to do it is to sauté the vegetables in a little oil, then add a little chicken broth to steam and then add salt. By "steam" I mean add ½ inch of broth in your pan and boil until the broth is gone. The healthy oil and broth provide plenty of flavor. By "steam" I mean boil the vegetables in the broth until there is no more broth left.   You want your vegetables to be crisp, not soggy.

Zucchini and Tomatoes

Sauté zucchini in a pan with 1 tsp oil. You can also add onion or scallions. Add ¼ cup water and steam until done. Add chopped tomatoes and Italian seasoning or just garlic and salt or rosemary and salt. Use two parts zucchini to one part tomato. You can expand this dish to include summer squash and yellow squash.

Coleslaw

Chop ¾ green cabbage with ¼ red cabbage. Add scallions, shredded carrots red onion and green pepper so your ratio is 1 part vegetables to 3 parts cabbage. Season with 4 parts mayonnaise to 1 part sour cream. You will need 1 cup dressing to 6 cups coleslaw. Add a pinch of sugar and a dash of vinegar and salt to taste. Add your seasonings. I like basil, others like celery salt and mustard. Experiment and create your own perfect recipe. You can refer to online recipes for ideas.

Bean Salad

I have a couple containers in my freezer that I add different beans to whenever I cook beans, so the container will have pinto, black, kidney and garbanzo beans. Then all I need to do is pull out the container and add chopped red onion, a green pepper, cilantro and tomato. To season I add lemon juice, salt and olive oil. Bean salad makes a great side dish or snack.

Baked Squash

I love baked squash and it is really filling. You can fill the center with rice and serve with a meal. Simply cut almost any squash in half or fourths and bake in the oven until you can put a fork easily through the meat. You can then add some butter and some brown sugar and grill it under the broiler.

Kale, Spinach, Garlic Side Dish

Sauté two parts kale to one part spinach in olive oil with a couple cloves of garlic. Salt to taste.

Grilled Vegetables

Thinly slice your vegetables. Brush with olive oil and salt. Either fry in a pan over medium heat or grill on the barbecue over medium heat. Vegetables are done when you can easily stick a fork through them.

Tempura Directions

Tempura is not inexpensive if you use organic oil and it takes time to make, so it does not fit with the theme of this book. So why am I including it, you ask? The answer is that I love fried food from time to time, so I make French fries and tempura to satisfy that craving. To prepare, thinly slice vegetables like butternut squash, yams, broccoli, summer squash and cauliflower to 1/8-1/4 inch thick. Dense vegetables like yams should be thinner. Green beans and shrimp also make great tempura because they are not "hard" vegetables like the first list, so you don't need to thinly slice. My favorite is squash tempura. What vegetables do you like? Those are the ones you want to use. Shrimp tempura tacos are awesome. You will need a high heat oil like sunflower seed oil. Most recipes recommend peanut oil because it is high heat, but organic peanut oil is expensive unless you purchase it in bulk.

The colder the batter and the hotter the oil, the crispier the tempura. If your batter is not cold and your oil is not hot, it will come out soggy. So make your batter and put in the freezer while you cut up your vegetables.

Heat your oil over a medium high heat. If you do this on high and the oil starts smoking, it is making a chemical that is toxic and your food won't taste right. Fry 6 to 8 pieces at a time until puffy and light golden, about 1 to 2 minutes. Remove to a cooling rack lined with paper towels.

Tempura Batter Ingredients	Organic Budget
½ cup sprouted brown rice flour	$1.00
½ cup millet flour	.40
¼ cup potato flour or cornstarch	.20
1 large egg, beaten	.40
1 1/2 cups cold water	
Tempura Vegetables	
Squash, Broccoli, Cauliflower, etc.	
Estimate $2 to $3 for the vegetables plus $2.00 for the batter for 4 servings is @ $1 to $1.50 per serving.	

CHAPTER NINETEEN

Let's Bake Gluten Free

If you are not used to eating gluten free products, then buy a gluten free pizza dough crust at your local health food store. Even if you are on a budget, you need to experience the texture of gluten free, so you will know if you made the one from scratch right. The deserts like blueberry bread will be similar to bakery goods you are familiar with, but not the dough products because gluten makes bread rise. Without it, the texture is different. Eggs make the deserts light, but you don't want a pizza dough that has the consistency of cake so you can't use a lot of eggs for your bread products.

This chapter will introduce you to the principles of gluten free baking. Throughout this book we have been teaching you principles, not just providing recipes. One great thing about cooking "gluten free" is that you don't need to worry about over kneading as there is no gluten to get tough. This chapter will outline what you need to know to produce awesome cakes and desserts, as well as baked goods like corn bread. If you have a sweet tooth, then this chapter is for you. Hopefully you will start substituting baked goods for candy and candy bars. If you eat high sugar candy and bars, it will wreak havoc with your health.

These baked goods will satisfy your sweet tooth and metabolize slower than candy because of the protein and fat, thus saving your pancreas and adrenals. However these are not foods you should live on. They are treats to be eaten in moderation. Try to form a habit of eating "muffin" type deserts, meaning no icing. The sugar content in icing is obscene. The whole grain goodness, organic ingredients and eggs, make these deserts truly healthy as opposed to "energy" bars that are full of corn syrup and white flour which depletes your system of vitamins and adds toxins to your body. In addition, you will notice that you are satisfied with less. Foods that deplete your system of nutrients will often make you hungry as your body will seek what it needs.

You will be using sprouted brown rice flour and sometimes sorghum flour, which tastes similar to wheat but has no gluten. Instead of yeast, you will use xanthan gum. To achieve the same texture as white flour baked deserts, you will be using additional eggs and more baking powder than you would normally use when cooking with "all purpose" flour because the flours in our baking mix lack the gluten rising component. If you have ever made a cake, the recipe calls for oil. Oil is heavy and while your baked goods will rise, they will collapse if you use oil with gluten free flour.

Butter and mayonnaise is lighter. With mayonnaise you will come closer to the texture of a real cake. However the butter adds a richer flavor so experiment and create your own "perfect" recipe. If you just reacted to the idea of including fat in your diet in the form of butter and mayonnaise, remember that because you are eating less meat and dairy, you are consuming overall a lot less fat. Eating one muffin or a serving of coffee cake that has butter in it, is not going to throw your fat intake out of whack, so enjoy. Also you need the fat to slow down the metabolism of the sugar so you don't exhaust your pancreas and adrenals.

If you bake a lot, then make up your own baking mix which will save a lot of time and money in the future. You can buy organic gluten free baking mix if money is not a concern, but it will be hard to find one that uses "sprouted" brown rice flour. I found the best price on organic potato and tapioca flour at Anthony's at Amazon. If you like chocolate and are willing to pay for bulk of 2-5 pounds from Anthony's, you will save 50% over purchasing organic chocolate powder when you buy it in smaller quantities. If you are willing to pay a little more, then get the Fair Trade, Dagoba cacao.

You will need 3 times more rice flour than tapioca flour and 4 times more rice flour than potato flour. I purchase 3, 4 pound bags of organic sprouted brown rice flour, 1, 5 pound bag of Tapioca and 1, 5 pound bag of Potato. You should have some potato flour left over that you can use for thick-ening sauces, for pizza crust and pastry crust. Potato flour also works well in cookies as you need a finer flour than the baking mix which can be a little coarse. I recommended sorghum flour for the nutritional value for the breakfast pancakes and waffles. However Sorghum can be a little gritty. If that doesn't sit well with you, then use a little sorghum and some millet flour which is a little finer. Both flours have great nutritional value.

If you want to divide the recipes in half or a third, etc., you can use this guideline: There are 8 ounces in a cup. 2 Tablespoons equal 1 ounce. So if you wanted to cut ¼ cup in half, you would need 2 tablespoons since ¼ cup is 2 ounces or 4 Tablespoons and you only need half that much.

Baking Mix

6 cups organic sprouted brown rice flour

3 cups organic tapioca flour – Adds "spring" to your baked goods.

1 cup organic potato flour – Adds a more refined texture.

1 TB plus 1 tsp salt

1 TB plus 1 tsp baking soda

4 TB aluminum free baking powder

1 TB Xanthan gum

Mix well and store in an air tight container.

Desert Budget

Cost of baking mix is $1.25 per cup. Cost of sugar is $1 per cup. The cost of an egg is 40 cents. One cube organic butter is $1.25 (1/2 cup) Mayonnaise is @ same price as half a cup of butter. Cookies are @75 cents for a 6 inch cookie. Total base price for a dozen muffins or 8 x 8 cake is @$8 plus cost of Stevia, berries or applesauce, cinnamon, etc., so figure @$10 per dozen or 85 cents per muffin plus frosting.

So let's estimate $1 apiece, but keep in mind that these muffins are low sugar, organic, gluten free. You would be lucky to find them at all and if you did, they would sell for close to $3 apiece.

Just letting you know the costs in case it is important for you to stay under $10 a day for food. Baked goods will throw your budget out of whack if you eat too much of these and they tend to be acidic. Cookies and muffins are meant as a treat, one a day. You will love the taste of whole grain baked goods!

Chocolate Chip Cookies	Oatmeal Cookies
1 cube butter	1 cube butter
1 egg	1 egg
1 cup baking mix	1 cup baking mix
½ tsp stevia	½ tsp stevia
1 tsp vanilla	1/2 tsp cinnamon
½ cup potato flour	2 cups oatmeal
1 TB brown sugar	3 to 6 TB milk
½ cup chocolate chips	½ cup raisins
½ cup white sugar	¾ cup sugar

Cookie Directions

Blend the butter stevia and sugar. Stir in the baking mix. Split into two bowls if you are making both recipes. Then add potato flour and vanilla in the first bowl and oatmeal and cinnamon in the second bowl and beat until blended. Taste it. If not sweet enough add more sugar. Then add the egg. Always stir flour in first before you beat or it will fly everywhere. Stir in the chocolate chips for the chocolate chip cookies. Add raisins and milk if you are making the oatmeal cookies. Do not beat or they will break up. Dough should be slightly wet. If too dry, add the milk 1 TB at a time. Put in a glass storage container and make one cookie per person. Bake at 350 for 8 to 10 minutes.

Granola/Breakfast Bars	Organic Budget
2.5 cups rolled oats	$ 1.00
¼ cup potato flour	.50
½ cup oil	1.20
½ cup honey plus 1 TB	.50
½ tsp Stevia	.10
½ tsp salt	.10
2 tsp Vanilla	.20
1 egg, (optional)	.40
½ cup raisins or other dried fruit like cranberries, nuts (optional)	.60
1 tsp Fair Trade cinnamon (optional)	

Total of $4.60 divided by 8 bars is @60 cents per bar or slightly more with nuts.

Peanut Butter Granola Bars

Substitute peanut butter for the oil and eliminate the flour and vanilla.

Directions for Granola Bars

There are many recipes for granola bars. Most use corn syrup or Karo syrup as both make the bars stick together. So does gluten. You will be using honey and potato flour to accomplish the "sticking together" aspect that you need. Warm the oil and honey together in a pan until honey has become a syrup. Stir before taking off the stove. It is too difficult to try and stir honey into a mix. By combining the oil and honey and heating slightly, it will be easy and save time. Combine the dry ingredients together. Add in the honey and oil and stir until everything is moistened. Taste to see if you need more sweetener. Cover the bottom of your dish with parchment paper. Now you need to decide if you want your bars to be crunchy or a little more like a breakfast bar. If you want crunch then spread ¼ inch thick and press down. If you want a breakfast bar, then add the egg and spread ½ thick and press down. The thicker the mix, the less likely it will crumble so you may need to experiment a little by adding a little more honey and potato flour if your "crunchy" version is not sticking together. Cook at 400 degrees for the crunchy version for 15 minutes. It should be slightly brown on top. If you are preparing the breakfast bar type, cook at 350 for 20 minutes. Cool and cut with a sharp knife. These can be constipating if you eat a lot of them. Just an FYI.

Blueberry Sour Cream Cake and Applesauce Cake

Since we are big on cooking two meals to save time, try cooking two deserts for variety. The second desert only adds another 10 minutes to your preparation time. Both require the same cooking time so as long as you are turning your oven on, create two deserts! Doesn't Sour Cream Blueberry Muffins and Applesauce Raisin Cake sound yum! If you don't want to make both deserts at once, then split step 1 in half.

Ingredients Step One	Applesauce Cake	Blueberry Sour Cream Cake
3.5 cups baking mix	1 tsp cinnamon	8 oz sour cream or plain yogurt
1.5 cups organic, fair trade sugar	½ tsp cloves	½ cup blueberries
1 tsp Stevia	¼ tsp nutmeg	¼ cup baking mix
4 Eggs	1 cup applesauce	½ tsp vanilla
½ cup butter (1 cube)	3 TB raisins	1 TB brown sugar
½ cup milk (coconut milk)	2 TB Flour	

Directions to Make the Cakes

Take the butter out and let it get soft while you are pulling out the other ingredients. Beat together all wet ingredients, milk, butter and eggs. Add the sugar and stevia and beat. Add in the flour and stir, then beat. Divide in half. In one bowl add the ingredients for the Applesauce Cake and in the other the ingredients for the Blueberry Sour Cream Cake. Beat separately then pour into either a greased muffin tin or an 8 x 8 greased pyrex dish. Best to use paper muffin inserts in the muffin pan and parchment paper on the bottom of the pyrex dish.

If making muffins, cook at 350 for 20 to 25 minutes. If making a cake in the pyrex dish, you need to increase the cooking time to 30 to 40 minutes. As you near the end of your cooking time test by putting a knife or toothpick in the center. If it comes out dry, your desert is done. If you overcook your desert will fall a little. Let cool and enjoy. After you have had a chance to taste, then adjust the recipe to your liking. Brown sugar works well with the Applesauce cake. If you could still enjoy these deserts and have them be a little less sweet, then use more stevia and less sugar as sugar is the only ingredient that is unhealthy and very acidic.

Under the section entitled "Fruit Glaze" are several suggestions for adding toppings to your deserts that are low in sugar. At first it may not seem that appealing but after a while you may prefer these low sugar toppings. If you have reached the point where frosting seems so sweet it is a little sickening, then you have retrained your taste buds to prefer food that is healthy and life building. Healthy bodies know what works. They naturally reject toxic, acidic food. Remember the first time you tried cigarettes or coffee. It was awful, right?!

White Cake

2 and ¼ cups baking mix

½ cup organic mayonnaise

¼ cup butter

1 cup organic, fair trade sugar

¼ tsp stevia

4 eggs

1 cup butter milk

2 tsp vanilla extract

1/8 tsp salt

Directions for the Cake

You can make this recipe, then split in half and make half white cake and to the other bowl, add ½ cup chocolate powder and 3 TB milk for a chocolate cake. The mayonnaise gives this cake the consistency of a real cake. If you can't find organic mayonnaise, then make your own using any recipe online using organic oil. Often commercial mayonnaise contains soy oil which is a GMO product and contains hexane. Beat together the eggs, sugar, butter and mayonnaise until fluffy. Add the rest of the ingredients except ¼ cup flour and stir, then beat. Depending on how large your eggs are, you may or may not need the extra flour. Batter should be thick, but easy to stir. If a little runny then add the extra flour, 1 TB at a time until you get the right consistency. Cook at 350 degrees for 25 to 35 minutes in a parchment lined pan.

Creative Toppings and Fruit Glaze

Rather than using heavy sugar frosting, you can use whip cream or coconut whip cream or you can try to make a fruit glaze. To make coconut whip cream, simply put a can of coconut milk in the fridge for an hour. Scoop off the thick milk on top and whip at high speed. To make the fruit glaze, combine ½ cup water, 3/4 cup organic fair trade, white sugar, ¼ tsp Stevia and bring to a boil. Turn off the heat and add in 1 tsp organic corn starch or potato flour that has been mixed in 1 TB water until dissolved. If you add the corn/potato starch into the hot liquid it will lump. Let cool and add in 1 cup sliced strawberries, peaches, etc. You can also use sliced apples. Just cook them a little so they are soft. If too watery, add more cornstarch. Fruit glazes only really work with a flat surface. So for muffins, instead of the fruit glaze, indent them before you bake and put a strawberry dipped in sugar into the indent after you have baked the muffins. Also try dusting the top with powdered sugar and adding strawberries or blueberries or both. You could also try using a standard frosting recipe which is below and just use 1 Tb per cupcake on top like a dollop. The sugar in the standard frosted cupcake will send you into a sugar spin and you will wake up the next morning feeling very tired or hung over.

Chocolate Frosting Ingredients

1/4 cup butter

1/2 cup unsweetened cocoa powder

1/3 cup milk

1 tsp vanilla

2 1/2 cups confectioners' sugar

1 tsp Stevia

Corn or Quinoa Bread

1.5 cups baking mix

1 cup cornmeal OR Quinoa

2- eggs

1 cup buttermilk (coconut milk)

½ cube or ¼ cup butter

¼ cup frozen corn for the corn bread

¼ cup organic Fair Trade sugar

¼ tsp Stevia

1 tsp salt

Directions for Frosting

Pull the butter out and let soften. Beat together the butter, milk and vanilla together. Add in the sugar and stevia and beat. Then add the cocoa powder and stir, then beat. You can store in an air tight container and freeze unless you plan on using the rest of the frosting in a week.

Directions for the Corn or Quinoa Bread

Take the butter out first and let it soften while you pull out your other ingredients. Add 1 TB vinegar to the 1 cup milk to make buttermilk. Wait five minutes for the milk to curdle. Beat together the wet ingredients. Then add in the dry ingredients and stir until moistened and then beat. Pour into a pyrex dish and cook for 30 to 45 minutes, depending on how deep your dish is. An 8 x 8 inch pyrex dish would be @40 minutes. Muffins are 20 to 25 minutes.

Pull out and stick a knife in the middle. The Cornbread/Quinoa bread is done when the knife comes out dry and the top is just beginning to brown. Note how long your cooking time needs to be for next time when you make this dish. You can try substituting millet instead of Quinoa which is also an alkaline grain.

Biscuits

¾ cup baking mix

¼ cup butter

1 egg

2 TB milk (optional)

½ tsp sugar

Desert Biscuits

1 tsp cinnamon

3 TB brown sugar

¼ tsp stevia

¼ cup raisins or other dried fruit

1 TB milk

Organic Budget

Baking Mix – $1.00   Butter – 75 cents

Egg – 50 cents

Total @ $2.50 for 6 biscuits or 40 cents per biscuit.

Directions for Biscuits

Take the butter out until it softens and cut the butter into the flour mixture with a pastry blender until the mixture resembles coarse crumbs. The pastry blender is pictured on page 93. If you don't have a pastry blender then dice the butter and smash it in by pressing down with a spoon. Add the beaten egg. Then using a spoon, press down and drag the spoon across the bowl making sure all the butter is mixed in evenly. If too dry, add the milk 1 TB at a time. Either roll out or put in a pyrex dish and pat down with your hand until you get 1/2 inch thickness. Cut out 4 to 6 biscuits using a glass to cut. Cook at 425 degrees in a parchment lined tray for 8 to 10 minutes. To make the desert biscuits add in the ingredients in the menu to the left. The butter makes the biscuits flaky, but if you don't want to eat so much butter then just use 1TB oil instead which makes a raisin cake I love. Bake this cake at 350 for 10 minutes.

Sandwich Bread

I invite you to go online and check out "gluten free girl" for bread recipes. They are perfect. I am not a bread maker and I certainly don't want to put a recipe in the book without the author's permission so if you are interested in becoming a gluten free bread maker, go for it. If you rarely eat bread and seem to be fine with gluten from time to time, then keep it simple and buy bread. However if you are eating it every day, you really should consider learning how to make great breads. Since there is no gluten, no kneading is necessary which means these breads are a lot less work and you don't need a bread maker. You can make gluten free bread in a bowl and will only need a bread pan to cook it in.

Pie Crust	Budget
3/4 cup baking mix	$1.00
½ cup white rice flour	.80
1 TB sugar	.10
1/2 tsp salt	.10
6 TB butter	.60
1 egg	.40
Total is $3 divided by 8 is @ 40 cents	

Directions for Pie Crusts

Personally, for those items that are time consuming to make like pastry crust for a pumpkin pie, I use organic "Spelt" pie crusts that I can purchase at Whole Foods for $2.50 or $1.50 on sale. Yes it is wheat, but it is wheat that is 5,000 years old, not the wheat derivative that we use today that is causing so many health problems. However I prefer the taste of rice flour pastry as it tastes more like white flour pastry, while the spelt definitely tastes like wheat. If you are feeling industrious, then make up several pie shells and freeze them in plas – tic freezer bags. If you can't find them locally, you can always purchase re-usable pie tins. It is easier to make up several, than try to make up pie crusts individually. Stainless steel pie crust pans are a little pricey, but they will last you a lifetime. You will need to buy them online. One of the reasons we are including a pie crust recipe is for when you need a top crust for a chicken pot pie or other similar dish.

Mix your dry ingredients together and then using a pastry cutter, blend in the butter. You can use the Earth Balance non-dairy butter if you wish. Whip the egg until foamy and add in with the pastry cutter. If you don't have an egg, then just add 3TB of milk or coconut milk with a couple drops of vinegar. Roll into a ball and chill for an hour. Then put between two sheets of parchment paper and roll out into a circle. Place in your pie pan and pinch the edge so it makes those attractive ridges. If you are doing this for the first time, then you might want to watch a video on You-Tube on how to make pie crusts. You can freeze any left-over dough. Always cook at 400 degrees for 5 minutes before adding any wet ingredients like for a fruit or custard pie or the bottom crust will be soggy.

Directions for Pumpkin Pie

Earth Balance makes an organic "expeller pressed" dairy free butter meaning the oil is not hydrogenated like it is in many margarines. You can google "why hydrogenated oils are bad for you" to get the full run down on why you don't want to be eating them. You need to add butter because most pumpkin pie recipes call for cream and the coconut milk is not quite rich enough. Beat your wet ingredients together with the softened butter. Add the dry ingredients and stir, then beat. Pour into the pie crust. Bake at 350 for 40 minutes or until set. As the pie cools it will keep setting.

The first time you make this, combine all the ingredients without the egg and taste it. Is it sweet enough? Is there enough spice, etc. Adjust and then note your changes for next time. Then add the eggs and beat together. If you don't have pumpkin pie spice, then use 1 tsp cinnamon and ¼ tsp cloves, ginger and nutmeg. If you have any left-over pumpkin filling, you can make pumpkin bread simply by adding 1 part baking mix to 3 parts pumpkin filling or 1.5 TB baking mix to ½ cup pumpkin filling plus ½ tsp sugar. It comes out like a pudding bread and is awesome if you like pumpkin. Bake the pumpkin bread at 350 for 25 minutes.

Dairy Free Pumpkin Pie	Organic Budget
1 -15 oz can pumpkin	$2.00
1 -15 oz can coconut milk	3.30
2 - 3 TB non-dairy butter (Earth Balance)	.50
½ tsp stevia	.15
½ cup sugar	.50
2 eggs	.80
¼ tsp salt	.05
2 tsp pumpkin pie spice	.20
Total is $7.50 divided by 8 servings is 93 cents plus 40 cents for the crust or $1.33 per slice	

End of the Week Breads

Every week I clean out my fridge and often find rice or other grains that have about a day or two left before I have to toss. Rather than waste it, I make breads out it that come out like the consistency of a date bread. Some have come out so good, that I make them on a weekly basis. For instance, I was trying to make a Persian rice dish. So I soaked, then cooked 1 cup rice with 1/4 cup lentils, 1/4 cup raisins and 2 TB of oil. It did not come out right. So I took that pot of rice and lentils and added 1 cup baking mix, 3 eggs, 1/2 tsp Stevia, 1/2 cup sugar, 1/2 tsp cinnamon, 1/4 tsp nutmeg and 1/4 cup milk and cooked it for 20 minutes at 350 degrees. My whole family loved it! I am sharing this to encourage you to experiment. What do you have left over at the end of the week? Some carrots, maybe. Then bake them into a bread. Grains, vegetables, fruit and nuts all complement each other so well, it is hard to go wrong with any casserole or "bread" combination so be adventurous and see what happens.

CHAPTER TWENTY

Chocolate Lovers

Chocolate is only slightly acidic and 1 TB contains 8.4 mg of caffeine compared to 75 mg to 150 mg for coffee. Chocolate contains Potassium, Copper, Magnesium and Iron. Chocolate stimulates endorphins, which means it will make you feel happier. It can strengthen tooth enamel, lower blood pressure and contains lots of antioxidants.(20.1) It should be clear by now that I love chocolate! The only problem with chocolate is that it is slightly bitter so it needs sweetener and it is the sweetener that will get you in trouble, making everything you make very acidic and high on the glycemic index. However the good news is that chocolate covers the slightly bitter taste of stevia so you can use a higher ratio of stevia to sugar for chocolate baked products, bringing down the detrimental effects of sugar. Brown sugar also mixes well with chocolate and is slightly lower in carbs and acidity than white sugar. So enjoy, just don't eat too much.   1 oz of a chocolate treat per day could actually be good for you.   Much more than that and you are now in the fattening, high glycemic/acid zone. Let's start by treating yourself to a cup of hot chocolate. Wisk 1.5 TB cocoa powder, 8 ounces milk, 2 tsp brown sugar and 1/4 tsp stevia and heat until hot.   Only 6 grams of carbs for the sugar and 12 grams for the milk. While the milk makes this somewhat acidic, the carb count is low for the glycemic index.

Look for the 5 pound container of Fair Trade Dagoba Organic Chocolate Cacao Powder that is $40 at Amazon. A cup weighs 2.2 ounces which comes out to @$1.50 a cup. Find a friend to split it with as this is a lot of coco. You can purchase Wholesome Sweeteners organic, Fair Trade powdered sugar for $25.59 for 6 pounds or a little over $4 a pound. Their organic, fair trade granulated sugar sells for @$2 a pound. The fat in the deserts slow down the absorption of the sugar, so your pancreas and adrenals are somewhat protected.   It is for that reason that many doctors will allow their diabetic patients to eat dark chocolate because dark chocolate is high in fat, low in sugar. We use Stevia to cut down the sugar that standard recipes call for by 25%, but it still tastes really sweet. All these recipes are made using cocoa powder because organic baking chocolate is hard to find and if you can find it, it is expensive.   The only difference between cocoa and baking chocolate is the fat. If your recipe calls for 1 ounce of baking chocolate, experiment with 3 TB of Cocoa Powder and 3/4 TB of coconut oil.

Your desert budget is as follows: Organic Vanilla sells for $2.50 for 4 ounces or 62 cents per ounce. There are 2 TB in an ounce. There are 3 tsp per tablespoon, so we will figure 10 cents per teaspoon. Organic Stevia by Wholesome Sweeteners sells for @$10 for 60 teaspoons or 16 cents a teaspoon. If you are making these recipes for a party, then use less Stevia and a little more sugar. Your guests may pick up on the bitter aftertaste of the Stevia. Much more fun to have them experience that what you made is similar to what they would find in a store, only you made it with organic ingredients.

Coconut Oil, Chocolate Almond Fudge Directions

I get requests for non-dairy deserts so here is a great one. However almond butter is more expensive than butter, so it is a little pricey but soooooo delicious, high in protein and very nutritious. If you use your food processor to chop up whole organic almonds for crunchy fudge, your cost for the almond part will be half of what almond butter costs. Simply combine all the ingredients and let set in your refrigerator for an hour until it hardens. You need to keep this fudge cold.

Coconut Oil, Chocolate Almond Fudge	Organic Budget
1 cup creamy almond butter or 1.5 cups chopped almonds	$7.00
1/3 cup coconut oil, softened	.50
½ cup sugar	.50
½ tsp Stevia	.10
½ cup cocoa powder	.75
Total of @$9 divided by 6 servings is @$1.50 per serving	

Standard Fudge Recipe-Organic Budget	
1 cube (1/2 cup) butter	$1.25
¾ cup confectioner sugar	1.25
1 tsp vanilla	.10
¼ cup organic half and half	.50
½ cup plus 1 TB cocoa powder	1.00
½ tsp Stevia	.10
Total is $4.20 divided by 6 is 70 cents	

Brownie Recipe	Organic Budget
1/2 cup butter or 1 cube	$ .75
3/4 cup white sugar	.75
¼ tsp Stevia	.05
2 eggs	.80
1 tsp vanilla	.10
1/3 cup cocoa powder	.50
1/2 cup baking mix	.75
Total $3.70 divided by 6 servings is 61 cents	

Fudge Directions

Mix together and heat on medium heat for 2 minutes. Then cool. It should set. If it doesn't, add more cocoa and heat, then cool again.

Brownie Directions

Melt the butter. In a separate bowl beat the egg and add the rest of the ingredients. Then add the melted butter. Line a pyrex dish with parchment paper. Add in the batter and cook for 35 minutes. Check at 25 minutes. If dry in the middle, it is done. If you want your brownies lighter, then next time use 3 eggs.

Chocolate Cake	Organic Budget
1.5 cups white sugar	$1.50
½ tsp Stevia	.05
1 3/4 cups gluten free baking mix	2.00
3/4 cup Fair Trade cocoa powder	1.00
4 eggs	1.60
¾ cup milk	.50
1/2 cup butter or ½ cup mayonnaise (lighter with mayonnaise)	.75
2 tsp vanilla	.20
1 cup hot water Total is $7.60 divided by 8 servings is @$1 per serving plus topping	

Cake and Frosting Directions

Preheat oven to 350 degrees. Beat the wet ingredients together except for the hot water. Add the dry ingredients. Then stir in the hot water. Pour evenly into two 9 inch pans that have been lined on the bottom with parchment paper. Bake for 30 to 35 minutes until a toothpick inserted in the middle comes out dry. Cool for 10 minutes before removing from pans.

Cream the frosting ingredients together. You can freeze your leftovers. To decorate the cake, experiment with creating a great presentation without using the standard ¼ inch frosting all over as that much sugar and fat is really hard on your body. Try using a pinch of powdered or colored sugar with a dollop of frosting and maybe a couple colored sprinkles. Use your imagination and have fun.

Frosting	Organic Budget
¾ cup cocoa powder	$ 1.00
6 TB butter	.75
2 cups powdered sugar	3.00
½ tsp Stevia	.10
2/3 cup milk	.50
1 tsp vanilla	.10
Total is $5.45 to frost a standard cake.	

References: (20.1) www.fitday.com/fitness-articles/nutrition/healthy-eating/6-health-benefits-of-dark-chocolate.html

CHAPTER TWENTY ONE

Pets, Cleaners and Lotions

Your Pets

If you can't afford to feed your pets organic dog and cat food, then do the next best thing. Make sure there is no corn in the food. Lamb and rice is probably your best choice. Lamb does have hormones and most lamb is "grain finished"," but overall lamb is often grass fed and for that reason lamb is often a better choice than cow. Rice is a much better choice than corn.

What really concerns me about the way we treat dogs and cats is the toxic flea treatments that are used. I wouldn't put any of them on my children, so why would I want to put them on my dog. You pet your dog and cat, don't you? Then the flea treatments get absorbed through your skin. There are lots of natural ingredients that repel fleas and you can google "organic flea treatments" to find them. I use Sentry "Natural Defense." which costs $7.50 for 4 treatments. Fleas and ticks are repelled by lemongrass, cloves and peppermint and those ingredients block the neurotransmitter octopamine which only is produced by insects. It kills insects almost instantly but not their eggs, so you have to bathe your dog and re-apply every 3 to 4 weeks. My dog smells great from using this treatment. I call him my "pumpkin pie dog." The first time I used the Natural Defense, I was sitting on my bed and the fleas jumped off on me and my bed! So use it outside. If you just bathed your dog, wait a day for their natural oils to disperse before applying any flea treatment as flea treatments can irritate dry skin. When you bathe your dog, first start with wetting their face and neck. Fleas can travel fast and if you start with their back, the fleas will run to their face and you might miss some of these as you can't use flea treatments on their face.

Another great way to get rid of fleas is to purchase "Pet Brewers Yeast." You can get 1000 tablets for $13 with a dose of 1 tablet per 10 pounds of body weight. People who use these tablets as a flea control, swear by it. It also acts as a multiple vitamin for your pet. You can order at 1-800-pet med. With all that being said, if your pet is allergic to fleas and develops a skin condition despite your best effort to rid him/her of fleas, you may need to use what your vet recommends until you can get the fleas under control and then go back to your non-toxic treatments.

If you have carpets, fleas and others pests may be living in them. First wash your carpets, this will drown them. Then all you have to do to make sure they don't come back is sprinkle baking soda and salt in your carpet. Vacuum once over to spread it. Then let sit for half an hour and vacuum up the excess. Fleas and most germs cannot live in a totally dry environment and what the baking soda and salt does is take out all the moisture. I recommend you do this before you bring a dog or cat into your house as once the fleas jump off and start living in the carpet they will start laying eggs. If this has already happened, then you may need to repeat the baking soda and salt treatment a few times. If you want to wash your carpet again, you will need to vacuum up all the salt and baking soda first so you don't make a paste in your carpet with the water, that will take a lot of work to get out.

Flea Biscuits

If your dog is outside a lot, another way to discourage fleas from using your pet as a host is to feed him/her biscuits with yeast and garlic in them as pests can't stand that smell. The brewer's yeast is filled with nutrients for your pet. Healthy/non-organic dog biscuits are very expensive, usually around $1 an ounce. The less expensive GMO soy and sugar biscuits are not healthy, so even if you are not concerned about fleas, it is a good idea to make your dog biscuits where you have control over the ingredients and it will save you money. Takes 5 minutes and you can cook with your casseroles.

Dog and Cat Biscuits	Directions for the Biscuits
1 1/4 cups chicken broth 2 cups sorghum flour or rice flour 1 cup cornmeal 2/3 cup brewers' yeast 2 TB garlic powder or 4 cloves garlic 1-2 eggs	Combine all the dry ingredients and eggs and slowly add the water. You want a dough that is like a bread dough, not too wet. Flatten with your hand. Cook at 375 for 20 minutes. Then put in an air tight container and let harden. The great thing about these biscuits is that your dog will love them. Your pet doesn't care if you didn't make them perfect, so don't worry about it if they are a little lumpy. If you want some for your cat you need to add ¼ cup water, as cats will eat them if they are chewy, but not if they are brittle.

Your Teeth

If you notice on tooth paste labels it often states that if you swallow, you need to call poison control. (21.1) Anything you put in your mouth gets absorbed into your body and the whole poison control thing makes me nervous, so I recommend that you purchase your toothpaste from a health food store or online to find toxic free ones.

Do you like to use mouthwash? Are you using a chemical mouthwash? If so, try a salt water rinse instead. Salt kills bacteria and if your gums are irritated or infected, it will help kill the infection. Obviously if the infection persists, you need to see a doctor. If your dentist is okay with you using a salt water rinse every day, then use very little salt as you will absorb some into your body and rinse with non-salted water to get the salt out. An even better choice is to use "Neem" mouthwash. Neem twigs have been revered by Ayurvedic practitioners for years as a mouth rinse. Most of these mouthwashes add a little Anise and Cloves for a great smelling breath.

Cleaners

Cleaners get absorbed through your skin. Even if you are using gloves, you are inhaling them and they are toxic. Your commitment to not having poison in your diet needs to extend to your environment.   Only use non-toxic, biodegradable cleaners like Simple Green. A great one that will clean mildew in your bathroom and most anything else is 1/3 vinegar, 1/3 dish soap and 1/3 water. Apple Cider Vinegar and water makes a great window cleaner. Baking soda is great for scrubbing pots. There are books that you can purchase for very little money that will tell you how to make non-toxic everything from cleaners to air fresheners. Don't worry about the "germ cleaning" aspect of cleaning.   Most soaps kill germs and germs cannot live very long on a dry surface. If you use "germ killing" cleaners the germs become resistant and can come back stronger which makes it difficult for your immune system to kill them. The CDC recommends against their use for that reason. (21.2)

The fact is that vinegar kills bacteria like salmonella, E. coli, etc. Heinz just came out with a "cleaning vinegar" that is stronger than household vinegar that you can use if you are concerned about germs. It is always a good idea to kill germs on surfaces, like doorknobs to avoid colds and flu but in my experience, if you keep your immune system in good shape by eating well and drinking pro-biotic drinks every day, your body will be strong enough to fight off most viruses. You can avoid the toxins in laundry detergent and clean your clothes using a magnetic system and never have to buy laundry detergent again. The system offers a 90 day money back guarantee so you can try it to see how it works for you. http://waterliberty.com/detergent/

Your Air

If there are cars going by anywhere near you, then consider purchasing an air filter that uses carbon filters as they filter out some of the pollution. Check to see if your heating and air conditioning system can use them and run your fan often. If you have small children or asthma, it only makes sense to live at least 5 miles from any freeway to reduce your environmental pollution. Indoor environments often have more pollution than outdoor environments, so investing in a good air filter system is a smart move.

Skin Lotions

Lotions that you put on your skin may have chemicals in them and pesticides if they contain food ingredients. Your clothes could also have chemicals that are being absorbed through your skin like the chemicals from dry cleaning and the formaldehyde in synthetic materials that is used to keep them wrinkle-free. I don't recommend letting your child sleep with his/her face buried in their teddy bear.

To avoid toxins, use organic food grade oils that will moisturize well because the molecules are small enough to get absorbed, rather than sitting on top of your skin. So "Go Italian" and mix water and a little olive oil (1/2 tsp) in your hand to wash your face. When you get out of the shower use organic coconut oil mixed with the water on your skin. Let your skin dry, do not towel off. It only takes a minute. I dry my hair while I am waiting for my body to dry. Peninsula Grove, Extra Virgin Coconut, Fair Trade Organic oil sells for $30 for 54 ounces or 55 cents an ounce at Amazon. You can use this oil for your hair, skin, etc. Given that coconut oil has a natural SPF of 4, this oil makes for a great moisturizer for a short walk.

You will find that if you stop using chemical lotions that may actually be drying out your skin, you may only need to moisturize once a day. What about when you just need "hand lotion" you ask. After I have had my hands in water, I use a little oil, rub it in and then wipe my hands on a towel to get rid of the excess. If you don't believe that most lotions actually dry your skin out, then do the "cracker test." Put a little lotion on a cracker and wait 15 minutes. If it actually moisturized, then the cracker should be limp, right! You might find that the cracker is actually more brittle, drier than before you put the lotion on. If you want a mask that exfoliates, tightens pores, etc. you can simply mix oatmeal and water into a paste. If you are looking for organic anti-aging cream, NYR Organic has a great line and they have many Fair Trade projects for their product ingredients.

What about sunscreen given that there is now new evidence that the parabens could contribute to cancer. You can purchase organic sunscreen which is a little pricey or you can make your own sunscreen using a combination of olive and coconut oil and non-nano zinc oxide. A nano particle will enter the blood stream but a non-nano is too large and will not. For that reason, non-nano is safer. For the cost of 3 oz of sunscreen that you can buy online, you can make a pound of your own. You just have to be very careful that you don't inhale the powder as it causes lung damage. You should wear gloves and use a paper paint mask. Amazon sells non-nano zinc for $15 pound or close to 48 TB. The recipe for how to make the sunscreen comes with the order or try "Wellness Mama." This is where your being a health advocate pays off as you will have friends you can split the order with.

Natural Insect Repellants

Did you know that there are flowers that mosquitoes avoid? Marigolds contain Pyrethrum, a compound used in many insect repellents. Ageratum or Floss flowers secrete coumarin, which is widely used in commercial mosquito repellents. There are many flowers like this that you can plant near your porch or garden instead of using chemical insect repellants or insecticides. Ask your gardener or google "Flowers that repel insects." (21.3) What about toxic weed killers that you are inhaling and tracking into your house. Burn Out and EcoClear are made from vinegar and lemon juice and work great. If you need to get rid of termites, there are many alternatives now that don't involve toxins, like orange oil.

References:(21.1)www.livestrong.com/article/167101-"What-are-the-harmful-ingredients-in-toothpaste?" By William Lynch 3.12.14

(21.2) www.cdc.gov. "Questions about Antibacterial Cleaning Agents, Acne Medication, and Probiotics"

(21.3) www.gardenguides.com "Flowering Plants that Repel Insects" by Katherine Kelly

CHAPTER TWENTY TWO

Be an Advocate for Healthy Food

The Food and Agricultural Organization of the United Nations (FAO) has determined that a significant percent of the world's diseases would be eliminated if people substituted quinoa for white rice. Their site posts Quinoa's nutritional attributes, touting quinoa as the only plant food that has all the essential amino acids which makes Quinoa the only grain that is a complete protein. It also has trace elements and vitamins. Quinoa can adapt to different ecological environments and climates creating what the FAO terms more "food security." Disease causes a lot of misery and is very expensive, which is making the poor even poorer. This fact behooves us to take advantage of any opportunity you might have to promote substituting quinoa for rice in the third world as that will make a difference in the quality of life for the planet.

You can talk up the benefits of eating healthy to your social network. You will then have friends to split bulk orders with and save money. Bring food to your work and share it. People associate "Health Food" with "rabbit food" and aren't even willing to begin to look into eating better because they assume they are not going to like it. Actually eating the food makes a more powerful impact than telling them about it. You could recommend this book if they tell you that eating healthy is too expensive or takes too much time. Think about it……As more and more people get diabetes and other diseases, the cost of medical insurance will go up as well as taxes for the increase in medical costs and for the increased costs for disability payments.

I don't know about you, but I don't think it is fair that people who take care of their health should have to pay for disability payments for people who smoke and don't take care of themselves. For people who are making an effort to stop smoking, cutting down on sweets, etc., I commend you. I am referring to the people who are being blatantly irresponsible for their health. Sometimes people aren't aware of the consequences of their actions or they just don't know what to do about their poor health habits and how to make it all work. Sharing what works for you can be a real contribution to those around you.

CVS is to be commended for no longer selling cigarettes. Instead, they have major displays promoting the sale of "stop smoking" kits. We need to support companies that take this kind of stand by making it a point to shop there. We need more leadership from our officials like the example of Michael Bloomberg, the mayor of New York who banned artificial trans-fat from New York restaurants in 2006. Immediately the fast-food giants swapped cooking oils and bakeries found alternative types of shortening. Even Crisco, got a new formula. As a result of Michael's leadership, the U.S. Food and Drug administration announced that is phasing trans-fat out of all food products. (22.1) A large part of Mayor Bloomberg's motivation was financial. He is trying to cut down on health care costs by making common sense decisions.

"Sugary drinks add about 200 calories a day to the average person's diet, contributing to obesity that in New York accounts for 5,800 deaths, including 1,700 from diabetes; 1,400 cases of end-stage kidney disease; and 2,600 amputations costing $4 billion a year according to Susan Kansagra, who heads the chronic-disease prevention and tobacco-control unit of the Health Department." (22.2) For that reason, Mayor Bloomberg also passed a law that outlawed drink sizes over 16 ounces. Of course, the Beverage companies sued and it got overturned. (22.2) A 32 ounce drink contains over half a cup of sugar. If someone sat in front of you and ate half a cup of sugar by the spoonful, most people would be a little disturbed. Yet, there are people who are drinking several sodas a day.

It is encouraging that more and more schools are banning sugary drinks. We need to make a law that kids under 18 cannot purchase soda or sugary coffee and energy drinks. The caffeine and sugar in many of those drinks are at such a high dosage that it is sending their heart racing. While the beverage companies have power politically, they don't have any power over individual businesses. Companies can eliminate soda and sugar caffeine drinks from their machines. Many government buildings have banned sugary drinks because they understand the cost of poor health.

"Moms Across America" is a group you could join if you are interested in becoming an advocate for healthy kids and healthy food. (http://www.momsacrossamerica.com) This group has taken on educating America on the health dangers of pesticides. Moms are the ones who purchase most of the food in any country. Given the purchasing power of moms, as a united group they can dictate what foods are distributed in any country. If there isn't a market for it, it won't be produced.

It is the willingness of people to pay the price to purchase organic foods that has motivated food chains like Ralphs, to not only have

an organic food section, they are now creating their own brands and because there is no middle man they are very affordable. So is the "365" product line that Whole Foods has established.

Given that one in four teens are on the verge of or already have diabetes, it is encouraging to see organizations like www.teensturninggreen.org for teens and www.projectgreenchallenge.com for students taking action for a healthier planet. Young people are attracted to causes and it is inspiring to see so many young people involved in raising awareness. (22.3)

Let's Be Responsible For Our Environment

The quality of our environment directly affects the quality of our food and impacts the food supply. Pesticides are killing the earthworms. Earthworms burrows into the soil, creating pores through which oxygen and water can enter and carbon dioxide can leave the soil. They play a critical part in the process of growing food. In the U.S., if we don't do something about limiting the insecticides we use so we stop killing our bees, we will literally lose our food supply. If that happens, it will be "game over." Wars have been fought over less. If you didn't see the cover story in Time Magazine at the end of the summer of 2013, you can Google "bee population decline" to get the latest information on this. Albert Einstein once said that if the bees disappeared, "man would have only four years of life left." Albert Einstein is not a whack job conspiracy theorist, so we need to pay attention.

We have already covered using re-usable shopping bags and as much as possible going "Plastic Free" to protect the environment. We need to take on reducing environmental toxins. Using the biodegradable cleaners mentioned in Chapter Twenty Two, both protects you from toxins and is doing your part to not add toxins to our environment. Don't you think toxic cleaners should be outlawed, I mean really! The manufacturing alone of toxic cleaners dumps an enormous amount of toxins in the environment as does their use. There is almost always a more natural solution. So bite the bullet and stop buying toxic anything, if you can.

End Labor Trafficking, the Importance of Fair Trade

Many people assume that because slave labor is illegal in their country, no products produced by slaves would be allowed in. That is not how it works. As a result of people in the developed countries purchasing products made by slaves, including many food products, 20 million people live in misery. If you would like to educate yourself more on this, take the survey at "Slavery Blueprint." You enter your zip, marital status, number of children, etc. I took the survey and my results were that in order to maintain my lifestyle, 44 slaves worked for me. Yikes! Even better go to the "Free 2 Work" website and use their drop down menu for spices, clothes, etc., and go through your house. You will find that many items in your house like spices were produced by slaves.

Talk it up and educate your social network. Many of our food products like sugar, coffee, tea, chocolate, wine, fish etc. are produced by slaves. The Maritime Executive is working to raise awareness of the fact that the fishing industry uses slave labor, making the men and boys work 18 hour days, keeps them in cages and buys and sells them. Enough people have written Hershey that they agreed to have 100% of their cocoa be Fair Trade by 2020. At the end of 2013, they reached a benchmark of 10%. (22.4) We need to urge all companies to clean up their supply chains. There is a

concern that if there was no more slave labor, the cost of products will go up. In his book "Ending Slavery" Kevin Bales makes the point that starving slaves are not productive. Paid workers are far more productive. At a talk I attended the speaker demonstrated that one company would only need to charge 32 more cents per Teddy Bear if they no longer used slave labor.

Whole Foods is to be commended for their "Whole Trade" line. Many small farmers cannot afford the cost for either an "Organic" certification or a "Fair Trade" certification, so they don't reap the benefits of being able to market their products as "organic" and "slave free." "Whole Trade" means that Whole Foods is vouching that the products produced by their farmers are "slave free" and in many cases also organic. We need more companies to take these types of actions, where they include justice and fairness as part of their corporate mission.   What if all companies looked to see how they could create a more "just" world in how they conduct business?!

Clearly poverty and global hunger are major contributing factors to Human Trafficking as poor people will often feel forced to sell their children to the Traffickers in order to pay off loans. According to Oxfam, climate change is the single biggest factor to winning the battle against global hunger. Oxfam is to be commended for their "Behind the Brand" petitions. So far they have succeeded in convincing both Kellogg and General Mills to cut greenhouse gas emissions in their manufacturing and production processes as well as in their agricultural supply chains. If hunger in the Third World and Climate Change are two issues that are on your heart, then go to their site and help them by signing their petitions under "Take Action." In the U.S., go to Oxfam America. This organization gets to the heart of the matter which is …… "Hunger isn't about too many people and too little food. It's about power." www.oxfam.org

Ideally if your faith community and schools were to host a table at their annual fairs to raise awareness regarding the importance of purchasing "slave free" products, it would mean a lot to all the children who will never reach adulthood because they are literally "worked to death." You could use the information at www.free2work.org and have at your table both products made by slaves and products that are not and where to buy them, especially food items because these are products that people use every day. Many people do not know what "Fair Trade" means. If enough people demand that their corporations no longer allow products produced by slaves, then millions of children will no longer be robbed of their childhood. We need to speak up and raise awareness regarding our food, our environment and justice for the planet.

Now that you have more energy, you might want to consider donating time to a cause. If Human Trafficking is on your heart then purchase the book entitled "How You Can Fight Human Trafficking, Over 50 Ways to Join the Fight." The book outlines what individuals, service groups and faith based groups can do to fight both sex and labor trafficking. The book has close to one hundred actions one can take to fight for justice and protect the innocent. It is a very worthwhile read.

Conclusion

It never ceases to amaze me how God has provided for everything we need in nature. There are so many foods that heal, plants that repel insects, plants that boost our immune systems, etc. We just need to recover our ability to use His many gifts.

References: (22.1) Huffington Post, "Bloomberg Trans Fat Ban In NYC Set Example For FDA" David B Caruso 11.08.13
(22.2) www.Bloombery.com/News "New York Soda Size Limit Statute Barred by State Judge."
By Chris Dolmetsch and Henry Goldman 03.11.13
(22.3) NY Times, "Diabetes on the Rise Among Teenagers," By RONI CARYN RABIN MAY 21, 2012 12:01 AM
(22.4) Global Exchange - Hershey's and Fair Trade: Is it a Victory? 7th May, 2013 - Posted by Zarah Patriana

ACKNOWLEDGEMENTS

I could go on for pages to acknowledge the many people who encouraged me and made suggestions for this book. Special mention should go to my son Jason who after doing his own research, came home one day and told me we had to eat everything organic, not just what I thought my budget would allow. My response was "we can't afford it." His response was "we needed to figure it out, because it is important." So I did. Jason's commitment to health and well-being inspires me to strive for the best with regard to my health. I also need to acknowledge my son Christopher who challenged me to figure out how to make the food taste great without using a lot of salt, sugar and artificial ingredients.

Without the encourgement of Marianna Wescott, there would be very few pictures in this book. She had so many great ideas for settings and how to arrange food and made the picture taking so much fun.

Zen Honeycuttt, founder of "Mom's Across America" supplied many of the resources I used. She has a personal stand of "Empowering Community Leaders to be Global Game Changers." I consider it a priviledge to call her a friend as she constantly challenges me to think bigger with regard to the contribution I want to make to the world.

Made in the USA
Charleston, SC
31 December 2014